Who Should Rea

We've all heard the scenario: the fam.
side "dig your own" gem mine. Junior finds a sapphire the size of a
peach and ends up on national television telling the world how he
will spend his fortune.

⊺ This book is for those who have read these stories and want
their chance to find their own fortune. It is also a book for
those who would enjoy the adventure of finding a few gems,
getting them cut or polished, and making their own jewelry. It
is a book for those people who want to plan a gem hunting
vacation with their family. It is a book for those who study the
metaphysical properties of gems and minerals and would like
to add to their personal collections.

⊺ This book is for those who would like to keep the art of rockhounding alive and pass it on to their children. It is a book on
where to find your own gems and minerals and on how to
begin what for many is a lifelong hobby.

⊺ This is a book for those who aren't interested in the "hidden
treasure map through mosquito-infested no-man's-land"
approach to treasure hunting but do want to find gems and
minerals. It is for those who want to get out the pick and shovel and get a little dirty. (Although at some mines they bring the
buckets of pre-dug dirt to you at an environmentally temperature controlled sluicing area.)

Many an unsuspecting tourist has stopped at a mine to try his or
her luck and become a rockhound for life. Watch out! Your collection
may end up taking the place of your car in your garage.

Good hunting!

This volume is one in a four-volume series.

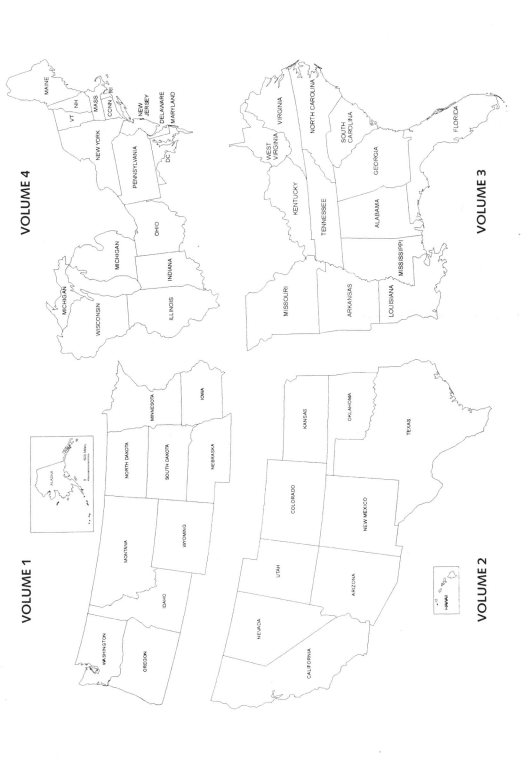

VOLUME 1

VOLUME 2

VOLUME 3

VOLUME 4

The Treasure Hunter's

GEM & MINERAL
GUIDES TO THE U.S.A.

4TH EDITION

Where & How to Dig, Pan, and Mine
Your Own Gems & Minerals

VOLUME 4: NORTHEAST STATES

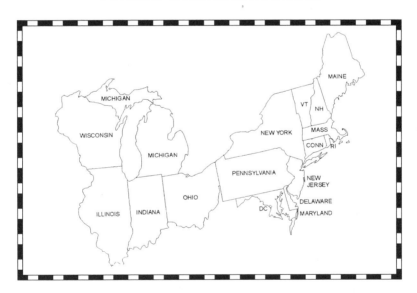

by KATHY J. RYGLE AND STEPHEN F. PEDERSEN

Preface by Antoinette Matlins, PG,
author of *Gem Identification Made Easy*

GEMSTONE PRESS
Woodstock, Vermont

The Treasure Hunter's Gem & Mineral Guides to the U.S.A.: 4th Edition
Where & How to Dig, Pan and Mine Your Own Gems & Minerals
Volume 4: Northeast States

2008 Fourth Edition
© 2008 by Kathy J. Rygle and Stephen F. Pedersen

2003 Second Edition
1999 First Edition
Preface © 2008 by Antoinette Matlins

For information regarding permission to reprint material from this book, please mail or fax your request in writing to GemStone Press, Permissions Department, at the address / fax number listed below, or e-mail your request to permissions@gemstonepress.com.

The Library of Congress has cataloged the third edition as follows:

Rygle, Kathy J., 1955–
Southwest treasure hunter's gem & mineral guide : where & how to dig, pan, and mine your own gems & minerals / Kathy J. Rygle and Stephen F. Pedersen—2nd ed.
p.   cm.
Rev. ed. of: The treasure hunter's gem & mineral guides to the U.S.A. c1999.
Includes index.
ISBN 0-943763-37-1 (NW)—ISBN 0-943763-40-1 (SE)—
ISBN 0-943763-38-X (SW)—ISBN 0-943763-39-8 (NE)
1.   Minerals—Collection   and   preservation—United   States—Guidebooks.
2.   Precious   stones—Collection   and   preservation—United   States—Guidebooks.
3. United States—Guidebooks. I. Pedersen, Stephen F., 1948– II. Rygle, Kathy J., 1955– Treasure hunter's gem & mineral guides to the U.S.A. III. Title.

QE375.R92 2003
549.973—dc21
                                                                      2003040801

ISBNs for fourth edition:

ISBN-13: 978-0-943763-55-2(NW)	ISBN-13: 978-0-943763-56-9(SW)
ISBN-10: 0-943763-55-X(NW)	ISBN-10: 0-943763-56-8(SW)
ISBN-13: 978-0-943763-57-6(NE)	ISBN-13: 978-0-943763-58-3(SE)
ISBN-10: 0-943763-57-6(NE)	ISBN-10: 0-943763-58-4(SE)

Cover design by Bronwen Battaglia
Text design by Chelsea Dippel

10   9   8   7   6   5   4   3   2   1

Manufactured in the United States of America

Published by GemStone Press
A Division of LongHill Partners, Inc.
Sunset Farm Offices, Route 4, P.O. Box 237
Woodstock, VT 05091
Tel: (802) 457-4000   Fax: (802) 457-4004
www.gemstonepress.com

Dedications, with love, to our parents and children:

To my parents, Joe and Helen Rygle, who taught me the love of nature; my earliest remembrances of "rockhounding" are hikes with my dad in the fields, forests, and streams near our home. I also remember weekend trips with my mother to a shop that sold specimens of minerals from around the world. To my daughter, Annie Rygle, who has shared with me the wonders of nature. Also, thanks to Annie for helping me sort the information for the first three editions. —K. J. R.

To my parents, Cliff and Leone Pedersen, who taught me to value nature and to not quit. To my daughters Kristi and Debbie, who challenge me to keep growing. —S. F. P.

To our combined families, including Georgia Pedersen, and to family no longer with us.

With special thanks:

To all the owners of fee dig mines and guide services, curators and staff of public and private museums, mine owners, miners, and fellow lapidarists. Our thanks to all those individuals both past and present who share the wonders of the earth with us.

To our agent, Barb Doyen, and her childhood rock collection.

To our publisher, Stuart M. Matlins; editors Emily Wichland, Jessica Swift, and Michaela Powell; Production members Tim Holtz, Jenny Buono, Kristi Menter, and Melanie Robinson; and all the staff at GemStone Press for their guidance, assistance, and patience.

To Mrs. Betty Jackson for, in her own way, telling Kathy to write the books.

To God and the wonders He has given us.

And finally, to each other, with love and the perseverance to keep on trying.

Volume 4—Northeast States

CONTENTS

State Listings

Indexes

Enjoying Stones

All-American Gems

by Antoinette Matlins, PG

When Americans think of costly and fabled gems, they associate them with exotic origins—Asia, South Africa or Brazil. They envision violent jungle quests or secret cellars of a sultanate, perhaps scenes from a Jorge Amado novel or from *A Thousand and One Nights*, a voluptuous Indian princess whose sari is adorned with the plentiful rubies and sapphires of her land, or a Chinese emperor sitting atop a throne flanked by dragons carved from exquisitely polished jade.

Asked what gems are mined in the United States, most Americans would probably draw a blank. We know our country is paved with one of the finest highway systems in the world, but we don't know that just below the surface, and sometimes on top of it, is a glittering pavement of gemstones that would color Old Glory. The red rubies of North Carolina, the white diamonds of Arkansas, the blue sapphires of Montana—America teems with treasures that its citizens imagine come from foreign lands. These include turquoise, tourmaline, amethyst, pearls, opals, jade, sapphires, emeralds, rubies, and even gem-quality diamonds.

Not only does America have quantity, it has quality. American gems compare very favorably with gems from other countries. In fact, fine gemstones found in the U.S. can rival specimens from anywhere else in the world. Some gems, like the luxurious emerald-green hiddenite and steely blue benitoite, are found only in America. Others, like the tourmalines of Maine and California, rival specimens found in better-known locations such as Brazil and Zambia.

The discovery of gemstones in U.S. terrain has been called a lost chapter in American history. It continues to be a saga of fashion and fable that, like the stones themselves, are a deep part of our national heritage. Appreciation of our land's generous yield of sparkling colored stones reached a zenith at the end of the nineteenth century with the art nouveau movement and its utilization of them. When the Boer Wars ended, South Africa's diamonds and platinum eclipsed many of our own then so-called semiprecious stones. Not until the 1930s, and again starting with the 1960s, did economics and the yen for color make gems more desirable again.

In the late 1800s, the nation sought out and cherished anything that was unique to the land. The search for gemstones in America coincided with the exploration of the West, and nineteenth-century mineralogists, some bonafide and others self-proclaimed, fulfilled that first call for "Made in America." Their discoveries created sensations not only throughout America but in the capitals of Europe and as far away as China. The Europeans, in fact, caught on before the Americans, exhibiting some of America's finest specimens in many of Europe's great halls.

But the search for gemstones in this country goes back even further than the nineteenth century. In 1541, the Spanish explorer Francisco Coronado trekked north from Mexico in the footsteps of Cortés and Pizarro, searching not only for gold but also for turquoise, amethyst and emeralds. In the early 1600s, when English settlers reached Virginia, they had been instructed "to searche for gold and such jewels as ye may find."

But what eluded the Spanish explorers and early settlers was unearthed by their descendants. Benitoite, which may be our nation's most uniquely attractive gem, was discovered in 1907 in California's San Benito River headwaters. A beautiful, rare gem with the color of fine sapphire and the fire of a diamond, benitoite is currently found in gem quality only in San Benito, California.

Like many of America's finest stones discovered during the "Gem Rush" of the nineteenth century, benitoite was held in higher regard throughout the rest of the world than it was on its native U.S. soil.

The gem occurs most commonly in various shades of blue. A fine-quality blue benitoite can resemble fine blue sapphire, but it is even more brilliant. It has one weakness, however: in comparison to sapphire, it is relatively soft. It is therefore best used in pendants, brooches and earrings, or in rings with a protective setting.

While benitoite is among the rarest of our gems, our riches hardly stop there. America is the source of other unusual gems, including three even more uniquely American stones, each named after an American: kunzite, hiddenite and morganite.

The story of all-American kunzite is inseparable from the achievements of two men: Charles Lewis Tiffany, founder of Tiffany & Co., and Dr. George Frederick Kunz, world-renowned gemologist. By seeking, collecting and promoting gems found in America, these two did more for the development of native stones than anyone else during, or since, their time.

While working for Tiffany in the late 1800s, Dr. Kunz received a package in the mail containing a stone that the sender believed to be an unusual tourmaline. The stone came from an abandoned mine at Pala Mountain, California, where collectors had found traces of spodumene—a gemstone prized by the ancients but which no one had been able to find for many years. Dr. Kunz was ecstatic to find before him a specimen of "extinct spodumene of a gloriously lilac color." A fellow gemologist, Dr. Charles Baskerville, named the find "kunzite" in his honor.

Kunzite has become a favorite of such designers as Paloma Picasso, not only because of its distinctive shades—lilac, pink, and yellow-green orchid—but because it is one of a diminishing number of gems available in very large sizes at affordable prices. It is a perfect choice for the centerpiece around which to create a very bold, dramatic piece of jewelry. Designer Picasso's creations include a magnificent necklace using a 400-carat kunzite. Although it is a moderately hard stone, kunzite is easily fractured, and care must be taken to avoid any sharp blows.

Kunzite's sister gem, hiddenite, is also a truly "all-American" stone. In 1879, William Earl Hidden, an engraver and mineralogist, was sent to North Carolina on behalf of the great American inventor and prospector Thomas Alva Edison to search for platinum. Hidden found none of the precious white metal but in his pursuit unearthed a new green gemstone, which was named "hiddenite" in his honor.

Less well known than kunzite, hiddenite is an exquisite, brilliant emerald-green variety of spodumene not found anyplace else in the world. While light green and yellow-green shades have been called hiddenite, the Gemological Institute of America—this country's leading authority on gemstones—considers only the emerald-green shade of spodumene, found exclusively in the Blue Ridge Mountains of Mitchell County, North Carolina, to be true hiddenite.

The foothills of the Blue Ridge Mountains also possess America's most significant emerald deposits. While output is minimal compared to Colombia, Zambia or Pakistan, the Rist Mine in Hiddenite, North Carolina, has produced some very fine emeralds, comparable to Colombian stones. The discovery was first made by a farmer plowing his field who found them lying loose on the soil. The country folk, not knowing what they had come across, called the stones "green bolts."

In August 1970, a 26-year-old "rock hound" named Wayne Anthony found a glowing 59-carat "green bolt" at the Rist Mine only two feet from the surface. It was cut into a 13.14-carat emerald of very fine color. Tiffany & Co. later purchased the stone and called it the Carolina Emerald. "The gem is superb," said Paul E. Desautels, then the curator of mineralogy at the Smithsonian Institution. "It can stand on its own merits as a fine and lovely gem of emerald from anywhere, including Colombia." In 1973, the emerald became the official state stone of North Carolina.

A California prize, the warm peach- or pink-shaded morganite, was named by Dr. Kunz for financier John Pierpont Morgan, who purchased the Bement gem collection for donation to the American Museum of Natural History in New York, where it can be viewed today. Morganite is a member of the beryl family, which gives us aquamarine (the clear blue variety of beryl) and emerald (the deep green variety of beryl). However, morganite is available in much larger sizes than its mineralogical cousins and is much more affordable.

Many consider the core of our national treasure chest to be gems like the tourmalines of Maine and California and the sapphires of Montana, gems that are mined in commercial quantities and have earned worldwide reputations. One day in the fall of 1820, two young boys, Ezekiel Holmes and Elijah Hamlin, were rock hunting on Mount Mica in Oxford County, Maine. On the way home, one of the boys saw a flash of green light coming from underneath an uprooted tree. The find was later identified as tourmaline, and Mount Mica became the site of the first commercial gem mine in the United States. The mine was initially worked by Elijah Hamlin and his brother Hannibal, who later became Abraham Lincoln's vice president.

The colors of the rainbow meld delicately in the tourmalines of Maine, producing some of the finest specimens in the world, rivaling in quality even those from Brazil. A 150-mile strip in central Maine provides shades of apple green, burgundy red and salmon pink, to mention just a few. Some stones are bi-colored.

Miners are kept busy in the Pala district of San Diego County, California, as well. California, in fact, is North America's largest producer of gem-quality tourmaline.

The hot-pink tourmalines, for which California is famous, began to come into greater demand in 1985, as pastel-colored stones became more and more coveted by chic women around the globe. Curiously enough, over one hundred years ago the Chinese rejoiced in the fabulous colors of this fashionable stone. The Empress Dowager of the Last Chinese Imperial Dynasty sent emissaries to California in search of pink tourmalines. She garnished her robes with carved tourmaline buttons and toggles, and started a fad which overtook China. Much of the empress's collection of fine carvings was lost or stolen when the dynasty fell around 1912, but artifacts made from California's pink tourmaline can be seen today in a Beijing museum. China's fascination with pink tourmalines lasted long after the empress. In 1985, a contingent of the Chinese Geological Survey came to California with two requests: to see Disneyland and the Himalaya Mine, original site of California pink tourmaline.

While the Chinese are mesmerized by our tourmalines, Americans have always been attracted to China's jade. But perhaps we ought to take stock of our own. Wyoming, in fact, is the most important producer of the stone in the Western Hemisphere. The state produces large quantities of good-quality green nephrite jade—the type most commonly used in jewelry and carvings. California also boasts some jade, as does Alaska. Chinese immigrants panning for gold in California in the late 1800s found large boulders of nephrite and sent them back to China, where the jade was carved and sold within China and around the world.

The U.S. is also one of the largest producers of turquoise. Americans mostly associate this stone with American Indian jewelry, but its use by mainstream designers has regularly come in and out of fashion.

Some of the most prized gems of America are the stunning sapphires from Yogo Gulch, Montana. These sapphires emit a particularly pleasing shade of pale blue, and are known for their clarity and brilliance.

The Montana mine was originally owned by a gold-mining partnership. In 1895, an entire summer's work netted a total of only $700 in gold plus a cigar box full of heavy blue stones. The stones were sent to Tiffany & Co. to be identified. Tiffany then sent back a check for $3,750 for the entire box of obviously valuable stones.

Once one can conceive of gem-quality sapphires in America, it takes only a small stretch of the mind to picture the wonderful diamonds found here. A 40.23-carat white gem found in Murfreesboro, Arkansas, was cut into a 14.42-carat emerald-cut diamond named Uncle Sam. Other large diamonds include a 23.75-carat diamond found in the mid-nineteenth century in Manchester, Virginia, and a greenish 34.46-carat diamond named the Punch Jones, which was claimed to have been found in Peterstown, West Virginia.

Each year, thousands of people visit Crater of Diamonds State Park in Arkansas, where, for a fee, they can mine America's only proven location of gem-quality diamonds. Among them is a group known as "regulars" who visit the park looking for their "retirement stone."

In 1983, one of the regulars, 82-year-old Raymond Shaw, came across a 6.7-carat rough diamond. He sold it for $15,000 uncut. According to Mark Myers, assistant superintendent of the state park, the stone was cut into an exceptionally fine, 2.88-carat gem (graded E/Flawless by the Gemological Institute of America). Myers says the cut stone, later called the Shaw Diamond, was offered for sale for $58,000.

Diamonds have also been found along the shores of the Great Lakes, in many localities in California, in the Appalachian Mountains, in Illinois, Indiana, Ohio, Kentucky, New York, Idaho and Texas. Exploration for diamonds continues in Michigan, Wisconsin, Colorado and Wyoming, according to the U.S. Bureau of Mines. The discovery of gem-quality diamonds in Alaska in 1986 initiated a comprehensive search there for man's most valued gem.

Many questions concerning this country's store of gems remain unanswered. "Numerous domestic deposits of semiprecious gem stones are known and have been mined for many years," wrote the Bureau of Mines in a 1985 report. "However, no systematic evaluations of the magnitude of these deposits have been made and no positive statements can be made about them." Even as the United States continues to offer up its kaleidoscopic range of gems, our American soil may hold a still greater variety and quantity of gems yet to be unearthed.

And here, with the help of these down-to-earth (in the best possible way!)

guides, you can experience America's gem and mineral riches for yourself. In these pages rockhounds, gemologists, vacationers, and families alike will find a hands-on introduction to the fascinating world of gems and minerals . . . and a treasure map to a sparkling side of America. Happy digging!

T

Antoinette Matlins, P.G. is the most widely read author in the world on the subject of jewelry and gems (*Jewelry & Gems: The Buying Guide* alone has almost 400,000 copies in print). Her books are published in six languages and are widely used throughout the world by consumers and professionals in the gem and jewelry fields. An internationally respected gem and jewelry expert and a popular media guest, she is frequently quoted as an expert source in print media and is seen on ABC, CBS, NBC and CNN, educating the public about gems and jewelry and exposing fraud. In addition, Matlins is active in the gem trade. Her books include *Jewelry & Gems: The Buying Guide; Jewelry & Gems at Auction: The Definitive Guide to Buying & Selling at the Auction House & on Internet Auction Sites; Colored Gemstones: The Antoinette Matlins Buying Guide—How to Select, Buy, Care for & Enjoy Sapphires, Emeralds, Rubies and Other Colored Gems with Confidence and Knowledge; Diamonds: The Antoinette Matlins Buying Guide—How to Select, Buy, Care for & Enjoy Diamonds with Confidence and Knowledge; Engagement & Wedding Rings: The Definitive Buying Guide for People in Love; The Pearl Book: The Definitive Buying Guide;* and *Gem Identification Made Easy: A Hands-On Guide to More Confident Buying & Selling* (all GemStone Press).

Introduction

This is a guide to commercially operated gem and mineral mines (fee dig mines) within the United States that offer would-be treasure hunters the chance to "dig their own," from diamonds to thundereggs.

For simplicity, the term *fee dig site* is used to represent all types of fee-based mines or collection sites. However, for liability reasons, many mines no longer let collectors dig their own dirt, but rather dig it for them and provide it in buckets or bags. Some fee-based sites involve surface collection.

This book got its start when the authors, both environmental scientists, decided to make their own wedding rings. Having heard stories about digging your own gems, they decided to dig their own stones for their rings. So off to Idaho and Montana they went, taking their three children, ages 8, 13, and 15 at the time, in search of opals and garnets, their birthstones. They got a little vague information before and during the trip on where to find gem mines and in the process got lost in some of those "mosquito-infested lands." But when they did find actual "dig your own" mines (the kind outlined in this book), they found opals, garnets, and even sapphires. They have since made other trips to fee dig mines and each time have come home with treasures and some incredible memories.

Upon making their second collecting trip out west, the authors purchased some lapidary equipment, i.e. rock saw and rock polisher. They first used them to cut thundereggs collected from a mine in Oregon. The next project was to trim the many pounds of fossil fish rocks they acquired at a fee dig fossil site. A sequel to this guide series is proposed to cover authorized fossil collecting sites, educational digs, as well as museums on fossils and dinosaurs. It will include such topics as where to view and even make plaster casts of actual dinosaur tracks. There are even museums where kids of all ages can dig up a full-sized model of a dinosaur!

Types of Sites

The purpose of this book is principally to guide the reader to fee dig mine sites. These are gem or mineral mines where you hunt for the gem or mineral in ore at or from the mine. At fee dig sites where you are actually permitted to go into the field and dig for yourself, you will normally be shown what the gem or mineral you are seeking looks like in its natural state (much different from the polished or cut stone). Often someone is available to go out in the field with you and show you where to dig. At sites where you purchase gem- or mineral-bearing ore (either native or enriched) for washing in a flume, the process is the same: there will usually be examples of rough stones for comparison, and help in identifying your finds.

Also included are a few areas that are not fee dig sites but that are well-defined collecting sites, usually parks or beaches.

Guided field trips are a little different. Here the guide may or may not have examples of what you are looking for, but he or she will be with you in the field to help in identifying finds.

For the more experienced collector, there are field collecting areas where you are on your own in identifying what you have found. Several fee areas and guided field trips appropriate for the experienced collector are available. Check out the listings for Ruggles Mine (Grafton, NH, volume 1); Harding Mine (Dixon, NM, volume 2); Poland Mining Camps (Poland, ME, volume 1); Perhams (West Paris, ME, volume 1); and Gem Mountain Quarry Trips (Spruce Pine, NC, volume 3).

Knowing What You're Looking For

Before you go out into the field, it is a good idea to know what you are looking for. Most of the fee dig mines listed in this guide will show you specimens before you set out to find your own. If you are using a guide service, you have the added bonus of having a knowledgeable person with you while you search to help you find the best place to look and help you identify your finds.

Included in this guide is a listing of museums that contain rock and gem exhibits. A visit to these museums will help prepare you for your search. You may find examples of gems in the rough and examples of mineral specimens similar to the ones you will be looking for. Museums will most likely have displays of gems or minerals native to the local area. Some of the gems and minerals listed in this guide are of significant interest, and specimens of them can be found in museums around the country. Displays accompanying the exhibits might tell you how the gems and minerals were found, and their place in our nation's history. Many museums also hold collecting field trips or geology programs, or may be able to put you in touch with local rock and lapidary clubs.

For more information on learning how to identify your finds yourself— and even how to put together a basic portable "lab" to use at the sites—the book *Gem Identification Made Easy* by Antoinette Matlins and A. C. Bonanno (GemStone Press) is a good resource.

Rock shops are another excellent place to view gem and mineral specimens before going out to dig your own. A listing of rock shops would be too extensive to include in a book such as this. A good place to get information on rock shops in the area you plan to visit is to contact the chamber of commerce for that area. Rock shops may be able to provide information not only on rockhounding field trips but also on local rock clubs that sponsor trips. There are numerous listings on the Internet of rock and mineral clubs. Among these are the American Federation of Mineralogical Societies (www.amfed.org), which lists member clubs, and Bob's Rock Shop (www.rockhounds.com), which has a U.S. club directory (supplied information).

Through mine tours you can see how minerals and gems were and are taken from the earth. On these tours, visitors learn what miners go through to remove the ores from the earth. This will give you a better appreciation for those sparkly gems you see in the showroom windows, and for many of the items we all take for granted in daily use.

You will meet other rockhounds at the mine. Attending one of the yearly events listed in the guide will also give you the chance to meet people who share your interest in gems and minerals and exchange ideas, stories, and knowledge of the hobby.

How to Use This Guide

To use this book, you can pick a state and determine what mining is available there, or pick a gem or mineral and determine where to go to "mine" it.

In this guide are indexes that will make the guide simple to use. If you are interested in finding a particular gem or mineral, go to the Index by Gem or Mineral in the back of the book. In this index, gems and minerals are listed in alphabetical order with the states and cities where fee dig sites for that gem or mineral may be found.

If you are interested in learning of sites near where you live, or in the area where you are planning a vacation, or if you simply want to know whether there are gems and minerals in a particular location, go to the Index by State, located in the back of the guide. The state index entries are broken down into three categories: Fee Dig Sites/Guide Services, Museums and Mine Tours, and Special Events and Tourist Information. Please note that the information provided in each individual listing is subject to availability.

There are also several special indexes for use in finding your birthstone, anniversary stone, or zodiac stone.

Site Listings

The first section of each chapter lists fee dig sites and guide services that are available in each state. Included with the location of each site (if available) is a description of the site, directions to find it, what equipment is provided, and what you must supply. Costs are listed, along with specific policies of the site. Also included are other services available at the site and information on camping, lodging, etc. in the area of the site. Included in the section with fee dig sites are guide services for collecting gems and minerals.

In the second section of each chapter, museums of special interest to the gem/mineral collector and mine tours available to the public are listed. Besides being wonderful ways to learn about earth science, geology, and mining history (many museums and tours also offer child-friendly exhibits), museums are particularly useful for viewing gems and minerals in their rough or natural states before going out in the field to search for them.

The third section of each chapter lists special events involving gems and minerals, and resources for general tourist information.

A sample of the listings for fee dig mines and guide services (Section 1 in the guides) is on the next page.

Tips for mining:

1. Learn what gems or minerals can be found at the mine you are going to visit.

2. Know what the gem or mineral that you're hunting looks like in the rough before you begin mining.

Visiting local rock shops and museums will help in this effort.

3. When in doubt, save any stone that you are unsure about. Have an expert at the mine or at a local rock shop help you identify your find.

Sample Fee Dig Site Listing

TOWN in which the site is located / *Native or enriched[1]* • *Easy, moderate, difficult[2]*

Dig your own   *T*
The following gems may be found:
• List of gems and minerals found at the mine

Mine name
Owner or contact (where available)
Address
Phone number
Fax
E-mail address
Website address

Open: months, hours, days
Info: Descriptive text regarding the site, including whether equipment is provided
Admission: Fee to dig; costs for predug dirt
Other services available
Other area attractions (at times)
Information on lodging or campground facilities (where available)
Directions

Map (where available)

Notes:

1. Native or enriched. *Native* refers to gems or minerals found in the ground at the site, put there by nature. *Enriched* means that gems and minerals from an outside source have been brought in and added to the soil. Enriching is also called "salting"—it is a guaranteed return. Whatever is added in a salted mine is generally the product of some commercial mine elsewhere. Thus, it is an opportunity to "find" gemstones from around the world the easy way, instead of traveling to jungles and climbing mountains in remote areas of the globe. Salted mines are particularly nice for giving children the opportunity to find a wide variety of gems and become involved in gem identification. The authors have tried to indicate if a mine is enriched, but to be sure, ask at the mine beforehand. If the status could not be determined, this designation was left out.

2. Sites are designated as easy, moderate, or difficult. This was done to give

you a feel for what a site may be like. You should contact the site and make a determination for yourself if you have any doubts.

Easy: This might be a site where the gem hunter simply purchases bags or buckets of predug dirt, washes the ore in a flume or screens the gembearing gravel to concentrate the gems, and flips the screen. The gems or minerals are then picked out of the material remaining in the screen. A mine which has set aside a pile of mine material for people to pick through would be another type of site designated as "Easy."

Moderate: Mining at a "Moderate" site might mean digging with a shovel, then loading the dirt into buckets, followed by sifting and sluicing. Depending on your knowledge of mineral identification, work at a "Moderate" site might include searching the surface of the ground at an unsupervised area for a gem or mineral you are not familiar with (this could also be considered difficult).

Difficult: This might be a site requiring tools such as picks and shovels, or sledgehammers and chisels. The site may be out of the way and/or difficult to get to. Mining might involve heavy digging with the pick and shovel or breaking gems or minerals out of base rock using a sledge or chisel.

Maps

Maps are included to help you locate the sites in the guide. At the beginning of each state, there is a state map showing the general location of towns where sites are located.

Local maps are included in a listing when the information was available. *These maps are not drawn to scale!* These maps provide information to help you get to the site but are not intended to be a substitute for a road map. Please check directly with the site you are interested in for more detailed directions.

Special Note:

Although most museums and many fee dig sites are handicapped accessible, please check with the listing directly.

Fees

Fees listed in these guides were obtained when the book was updated, and may have changed. They are included to give you at least a general idea of the costs you will be dealing with. Please contact the site directly to confirm charges.

Many museums have discounts for members and for groups, as well as special programs for school groups. Please check directly with the institution for information. Many smaller and/or private institutions have no fee, but do appreciate donations to help meet the costs of staying open.

Many sites accept credit cards; some may not. Please check ahead for payment options if this is important.

Requesting Information by Mail

When requesting information by mail, it is always appreciated if you send a SASE (self-addressed stamped envelope) along with your request. Doing this will often speed up the return of information.

Equipment and Safety Precautions

Equipment

The individual sites listed in these guides often provide equipment at the mine. Please note that some fee dig sites place limitations on the equipment you can use at their site. Those limitations will be noted where the information was available. Always abide by the limitations; remember that you are a guest at the site.

On the following pages are figures showing equipment for rockhounding. Figures A and B identify some of the equipment you may be told you need at a site. Figure C shows material needed to collect, package, transport, and record your findings. Figure D illustrates typical safety equipment.

Always use safety glasses with side shields or goggles when you are hammering or chiseling. Chips of rock or metal from your tools can fly off at great speed in any direction when hammering. Use gloves to protect your hands as well.

Other useful tools not shown include an ultraviolet hand lamp, and a hand magnifier.

Not pictured, but something you don't want to forget, is your camera. You may also want to bring along your video camera to record that "big" find, no matter what it might be.

Not pictured, but to be considered: knee pads and seat cushions.

FIGURE A

1. Crowbar
2. Pry bar
3. Smaller pick
4. Rock pick
5. Various-sized chisels (*Note:* When working with a hammer and chisel, you may want to use a chisel holder, not shown, for protecting your hand if you miss. Always use eye protection with side shields and gloves!)
6. Rock hammer (*Note:* Always use eye protection.)
7. 3-pound hammer (*Note:* Always use eye protection.)
8. Sledgehammer (*Note:* When working with a sledgehammer, wear hard-toed boots along with eye protection.)

Other Safety Precautions

- Never go into the field or on an unsupervised site alone. With protective clothing, reasonable care, proper use of equipment, and common sense, accidents should be avoided, but in the event of an illness or accident, you always want to have someone with you who can administer first aid and call for or seek help.
- Always keep children under your supervision.
- Never enter old abandoned mines or underground diggings!
- Never break or hammer rocks close to another person!

FIGURE B

9. Garden trowel
10. Camp shovel
11. Long-handled shovels
12. Garden cultivators
13. Screwdrivers

14. Bucket of water
15. (Plastic) jug of water
16. Squirt bottle of water; comes in handy at many of the mines to wash off rocks so you can see if they are or contain gem material

FIGURE C

17. Backpack
18. Waist pack to hold specimens
19. Bucket to hold specimens
20. Coffee can to hold specimens
21. Boxes to pack, transport, and ship specimens
22. Bags—various sized bags to carry collected specimens in the field
23. Newspaper to wrap specimens for transport
24. Egg cartons to transport delicate specimens
25. Empty film canisters to hold small specimens
26. Plastic box with dividers to hold small specimens
27. Margarine containers to hold small specimens

28. Reclosable plastic bags to hold small specimens
29. Gummed labels to label specimens (Whether you are at a fee dig site or with a guide, usually there will be someone to help you identify your find. It is a good idea to label the find when it is identified so that when you reach home, you won't have boxes of unknown rocks.)
30. Waterproof marker for labeling
31. Field log book to make notes on where specimens were found
32. Sketching pencils, sketchbook (waterproof notebooks are available), paint to record your finds and the surrounding scenery

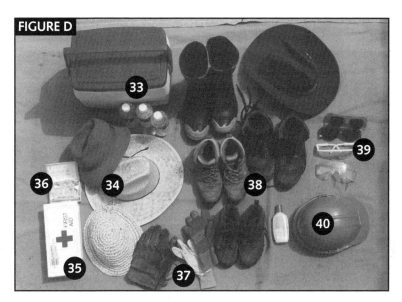

FIGURE D

33. Food and water—always carry plenty of drinking water (*Note:* many sites tell you in advance if they have food and water available or if you should bring some; however, it is always a good idea to bring extra drinking water. Remember—if you bring it in, pack it back out.)

34. Hats. Many of the sites are in the open, and the summer sun can be hot and dangerous to unprotected skin. Check with the site to see if they have any recommendations for protective clothing. Also, don't forget sunscreen.

35. First aid/safety kit

36. Snakebite kit. If the area is known to have snakes, be alert and take appropriate safety measures, such as boots and long pants. (*Note:* while planning our first gem-hunting trip, we read that the first aid kit should contain a snakebite kit. Just like rockhounds, snakes seem to love rocky areas!) In most cases, if you visit sites in the book, you will be either at a

flume provided by the facility, or with an experienced guide. At the first, you will most likely never see a snake; at the second, your guide will fill you in on precautions. For listings where you will be searching on a ranch or state park, ask about special safety concerns such as snakes and insects when you pay your fee. These sites may not be for everyone.

37. Gloves to protect your hands when you are working with sharp rock or using a hammer or chisel

38. Boots—particularly important at sites where you will be doing a lot of walking, or walking on rocks

39. Safety glasses with side shields, or goggles. Particularly important at hard rock sites or any site where you or others may be hitting rocks. Safety glasses are available with tinted lenses for protection from the sun.

40. Hard hats—may be mandatory if you are visiting an active quarry or mine; suggested near cliffs

Mining Techniques

How to Sluice for Gems

This is the most common technique used at fee dig mines where you buy a bucket of gem ore (gem dirt) and wash it at a flume.

1. Place a quantity of the gem ore in the screen box, and place the screen box in the water. Use enough gem ore to fill the box about a third.

2. Place the box in the water, and shake it back and forth, raising one side, then the other, so that the material in the box moves back and forth. What you are doing is making the stones move around in the screen box, while washing dirt and sand out of the mixture.

3. After a minute or two of washing, take the screen box out of the flume, and let it drain. Look through the stones remaining in the screen box for your treasure. If you're not sure about something, ask one of the attendants.

4. When you can't finding anything more, put the box back in the flume and wash it some more, then take it out and search again.

Clockwise from top: Gold pan; screen box used for sluicing; screen box used for screening.

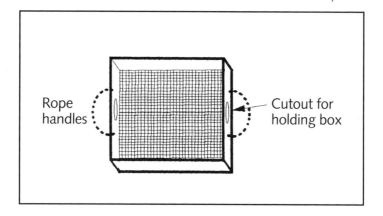

Rope handles

Cutout for holding box

How to Build a Screen Box

1. A screen box that is easy to handle is generally built from 1" x 4" lumber and window screening.

2. Decide on the dimensions of the screen box you want, and cut the wood accordingly. Dimensions generally run from 12" x 12" up to 18" x 18". Remember that the end pieces will overlap the side pieces, so cut the end pieces 1½" longer.

3. There are two alternative methods of construction. In one, drill pilot holes in the end pieces, and use wood screws to fasten the end pieces to the side pieces. In the other, use angle irons and screws to attach the ends and sides.

4. Cut the screening to be ¼" smaller than the outside dimensions of the screen box, and use staples to attach the screen to the bottom of the box. Use metal screening rather than plastic if possible. For a stronger box, cut ¼" or ⅜" hardware cloth to the same dimensions as the screening, and staple the hardware cloth over the screening. The hardware cloth will provide support for the screening.

5. Cut ¼" wood trim to fit, and attach it to the bottom of the box to cover the edges of the screening and hardware cloth and staples.

6. If you like, add rope handles or cut handholds in the side pieces for easier handling.

5. If possible, move your screen box into bright light while you are searching, since the gems and minerals often show up better in bright light.

How to Screen for Gems

This is another common technique used at fee dig mines where you buy a bucket of gem ore and screen it for gems. (The authors used this technique for garnets and sapphires in Montana.)

1. Place a quantity of the gem ore in the screen box, and place the screen box in the water. Use enough gem dirt to fill the box about a third.

2. Place the box in the water, and begin tipping it back and forth, raising one side, then the other, so that the material in the box moves back and forth. What you are doing is making the gemstones, which are heavier than the rock and dirt, move into the bottom center of the screen box while at the same time washing dirt and sand out of the mixture.

3. After a minute or two, change the direction of movement to front and back.

4. Repeat these two movements (Steps 2 and 3) three or four times.

5. Take the box out of the water and let it drain, then place a board on top and carefully flip the box over onto the sorting table. It may be helpful to put a foam pad in the box, then put the board over it. This helps keep the stones in place when you flip the box. If you have done it right, the gemstones will be found in the center of the rocks dumped onto the board. Use tweezers to pick the rough gemstones out of the rocks, and place them in a small container.

How to Pan for Gold

The technique for panning for gold is based on the fact that gold is much heavier than rock or soil. Gently washing and swirling the gold-bearing soil in a pan causes the gold to settle to the bottom of the pan. A gold pan has a flat bottom and gently slanting sides. Some modern pans also have small ridges or rings around the inside of the pan on these slanting sides. As the soil is washed out of the pan, the gold will slide down the sides, or be caught on the ridges and stay in the pan. Here's how:

1. Begin by filling the pan with ore, about ⅔ to ¾ full.

2. Put your pan in the water, let it gently fill with water, then put the pan under the water surface. Leave the pan in the water, and mix the dirt around in the pan, cleaning and removing any large rocks.

3. Lift the pan out of the water, then gently shake the pan from side to side while swirling it at the same time. Do this for 20–30 seconds to get the gold settled to the bottom of the pan.

4. Still holding the pan out of the water, continue these motions while tilting the pan so that the dirt begins to wash out. Keep the angle of the pan so that the crease (where the bottom and sides meet) is the lowest point.

5. When there is only about a tablespoon of material left in the pan, put about ½ inch of water in the pan, and swirl the water over the remaining material. As the top material is moved off, you should see gold underneath.

6. No luck? Try again at a different spot.

Notes on Gem Faceting, Cabbing, and Mounting Your Finds

Many of the fee dig sites offer services to cut and mount your finds. Quality and costs vary. Trade journals such as *Lapidary Journal* and *Rock & Gem* (available at most large bookstores or by subscription) list suppliers of these services, both in the United States and overseas. Again, quality and cost vary. Local rock and gem shops in your area may offer these services, or it may be possible to work with a local jeweler. Your local rock club may be able to provide these services or make recommendations.

After their first gem-hunting trip, the authors had some of their finds faceted and cabochoned. They then designed rings and had them made using these stones, as shown in the photos below.

After saying for years that they would like to learn to cabochon and facet (and in the process learn how better to collect "usable" material), the authors were fortunate enough to meet a local gemologist at a gem and mineral show who taught classes in the lapidary arts. They have since cut their own cabo-

The authors sent their rough gems away for faceting. Using the faceted gems, they made crude mock-ups and sketches of the rings they wanted; then they sent the mock-ups, sketches, and gems to be made into rings.

The finished rings.

chons and faceted gemstones, getting a true appreciation for the art and knowledge of what to look for when field collecting.

Cutting your own finds can be a very rewarding hobby, and this hobby works two ways. You can cabochon, facet, and carve your special finds to your specifications, then make or have them made into jewelry. A cabochon is a highly polished convex-cut, but unfaceted gem. Facets are flat faces on geometric shapes which are cut into a rough gemstone in order to improve their appearance. The angles used for each facet affect the appearance of the gemstone. In learning the lapidary procedures, you also gain knowledge of what is a good find. You can look at a stone in the field and see if it is facetable, or if the pattern would make a spectacular cabochon.

Understanding what beautiful pieces you can make from your discoveries will amaze you, be they dug from a native mine, sluiced at a salted site, purchased from a local rock shop, or traded at a club meeting.

The first step to learning the lapidary arts is to do some research to see if it is for you. Search out books and articles on the topic and contact local club or rock shops to see if there are any classes near you.

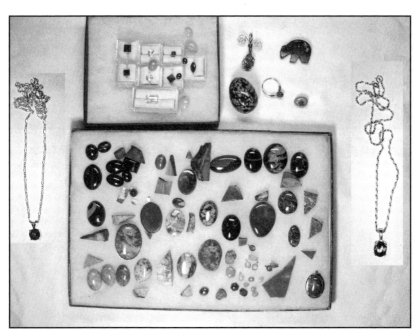

A sample of the authors' lapidary work.

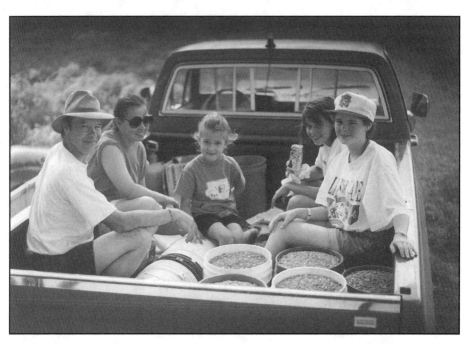

Taking sifted gravel to the jig at a sapphire mine in Montana. Pictured from left to right: Steve, Kathy, Annie Rygle, Debra Pedersen, Kristin Pedersen.

CONNECTICUT

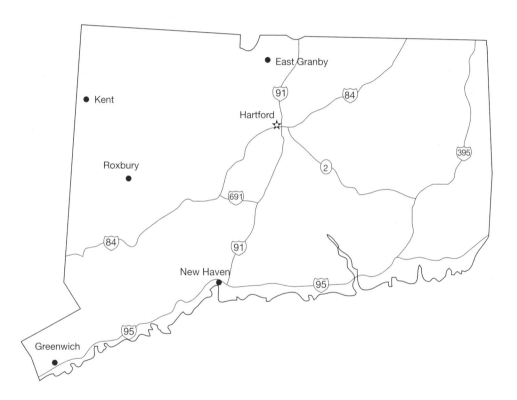

State Gemstone: Garnet (1977)

ROXBURY / *Native • Easy*

Find Your Own Garnets *T*

The following gems or minerals can be found:

• Garnets

Green's Farm Garnet Mine
Perkins Road
Roxbury, CT 06783

Open: All year, weather permitting.
Info: This is an unattended fee dig site. You leave your fee at the green house (leave the fee under the mat if no one is home). There is a parking area near the house; search for garnets in the old mine workings north of the parking area.
Admission: $2.00.

Directions: Maps and directions are available for sale on the Internet (search for Green's Farm Garnet Mine). Take I-84 east to Route 7 north. Take Route 7 north to Route 25 south. Take Route 25 south for a mile, and take Route 133 north for 6 miles, then look for Stuart Road on the right. Turn right on Stuart Road, and follow it (names may change) through Roxbury Falls. Another road branches to the right at Roxbury Falls; stay left, and look for Perkins Road on the left. Take Perkins Road; it will bend to the left, then go into an old farm, where there will be a newer house on the right, with a small parking area in front. Pay the fee at the newer house.

EAST GRANBY

Mine Tour/Museum

Old New-Gate Prison and
Copper Mine
115 Newgate Road
East Granby, CT 06026
Phone: (860) 653-3563

Off-season: (860) 256-2800
Fax: (860) 566-5078
www.cultureandtourism.org
(Click on "History" at top of page, then click on "Museums.")

Open: May through October, 10:00 A.M.– 4:30 P.M., Wednesday–Sunday.
Info: The Old New-Gate Prison and Copper Mine, formerly the Simsbury

Copper Mine, was the first American copper mine, chartered in 1707. Ore from the Simsbury Copper Mine averaged about 12% copper and in some cases ran as high as 50% copper. In the 1750s, work at the mine ceased because of several factors, including the expense of shipping ore to England for smelting.

In December 1773, the mine became a prison. Other copper mines existed near New-Gate, one of which was the Higley Mine. Between 1729 and 1737, Dr. Samuel Higley designed the first copper coins used for trading purposes in the country.

Miners followed the ore-bearing strata, which tipped two percent to the east, so at the lowest point of the tour, visitors are seventy feet underground. Tours at the mine tunnels are self-guided. When in the mine tunnels, be aware that the ceilings are sometimes low. The temperature stays in the low-50s, and a sweater is recommended, along with good walking shoes.

Admission: Adults $5.00, seniors $4.00, children (6–17) $3.00, children under 6 free. Special arrangements for groups, by appointment only.

Other services available: Picnic area, gift shop, and ample free parking.

Directions: From exit 40 on I-91, take Route 20W through East Granby Center to traffic light at Newgate Road. Turn right on Newgate, and drive 1 mile to mine. From Routes 10/202, take Route 20E from Granby Center for 2.8 miles

to the light at Newgate Road in East Granby. Turn left on Newgate, and drive 1 mile to the mine.

GREENWICH

Museum

Bruce Museum of Arts and Sciences
One Museum Drive
Greenwich, CT 06830-7100
Phone: (203) 869-0376
Fax: (203) 869-0963
www.brucemuseum.org

Open: All year, 10:00 A.M.–5:00 P.M., Tuesday–Saturday. Sunday 1:00 P.M.–5:00 P.M. Closed Monday.

Info: Exhibits of minerals and rocks are on display, including minerals from around the world, touchable meteorite, and minerals that glow in the "dark."

Admission: Adults $7.00, seniors (65+) and students (5–22) $6.00. On Tuesdays, admission is free.

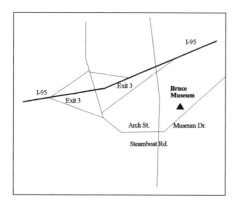

Directions: Take exit 3 off I-95. At the end of the ramp, turn east on Arch Street, and drive to the intersection with Steamboat Road. Go straight across to Museum Drive, and the museum will be 500 feet on the left. The museum is also easily accessible via the Greenwich train station on Metro North's New Haven Line.

KENT

Museum 🏛

Museum of Mining and Mineral Science
Connecticut Antique Machinery
Association
P.O. Box 425
Kent, CT 06757
Phone: (860) 927-0050
www.ctamachinery.com

Open: May–October, Wednesday–Sunday 10:00 A.M.–4:00 P.M., or by appointment.
Info: Connecticut had deposits of iron, copper, garnet, marble limestone, and other rocks, which drove the early indus-

trial activities in the state. The museum is located in an old iron-making area, with a historic iron furnace located nearby. The museum has a collection of Connecticut minerals, displays on geology, and on how the local Native American population used the local mineral resources.
Admission: Adults $3.00, children under 12 free.
Directions: Located in Kent on Highway U.S. Route 7. Shares a common driveway with the Sloane-Stanley Museum.

NEW HAVEN

Museum 🏛

Peabody Museum of Natural History
Yale University
P.O. Box 208118
170 Whitney Avenue
New Haven, CT 06520
Phone: (203) 432-5050
Fax: (203) 432-9816
www.peabody.yale.edu

Open: All year except major holidays, 10:00 A.M.–5:00 P.M. Monday–Saturday, 12:00–5:00 P.M. Sunday. Groups must register in advance.
Info: New permanent Hall of Minerals, Earth and Space, Phase I, opened in 2006. On display in the exhibit on earth and the solar system are pieces of moon rocks and meteorites. Gemstones and jewelry from private collections are on display. Phase 2

opens in the fall of 2008. It will have a new permanent mineral exhibit highlighting Connecticut geology, and the diversity of minerals, ores, fluorescent minerals, and gemstones. This exhibit will showcase Peabody's specimens, many of which have not been on display for decades. The study of minerals at Yale began with Silliman and was carried on by luminaries such as James Dwight Dana, the Yale professor generally acknowledged as the founder of modern mineralogy. Exhibits show how minerals form and grow, why crystals have such alluring shapes and colors, and how to use practices of mineral identification.

Admission: Adults $7.00, seniors over 65 $6.00, and children (3–18) $5.00.

Directions: For directions, call (203) 432-5050.

SECTION 3: Special Events and Tourist Information

TOURIST INFORMATION

State Tourist Agency

Connecticut Office of Tourism
1 Financial Plaza
755 Main Street
Hartford, CT 06103

Phone: (888) CTVISIT;
(888)-288-4746
Fax: (860) 270-8077
www.ctbound.org

DELAWARE

State Stone/Rock: Sillimanite

WILMINGTON / *Native ▪ Easy to Moderate*

Collect Common Minerals from Tailings Piles

The following gems and minerals may be found:

▪ Feldspar, quartz, garnet, and beryl

Woodlawn Quarry
Woodlawn Trustees
1020 N. Bancroft Parkway
Wilmington, DE 19805
Phone: (302) 655-6209
www.dge.udel.edu/Geology/
GeoAdventures/woodlawn.aspx

Open: Generally open during daylight hours.

Info: The quarry is located in a wildlife preserve owned and managed by the Woodlawn Trustees. You must obtain permission from the trustees before visiting this site. You cannot dig at this site, but you are allowed to look through the two tailings piles at the old quarry and pick up specimens. The quarry was active from 1850–1920 for quarrying feldspar.

Rates: Free.

Directions: Off Ramsey Road, near Brandy Creek State Park. A map can be found at the website.

> The Delaware Geological Survey has a series of Geo Adventures, which are designed to allow one to learn about a particular geologic point of interest in Delaware's Piedmont or Coastal Plain provinces and then take a short field trip to that area. You can find information on these Geo Adventures on the Survey's website: http://www.dgs.udel.edu/Geology/GeoAdventures/index.aspx.

SECTION 2: Museums and Mine Tours

NEWARK

Museum

Iron Hill Museum
1355 Old Baltimore Pike
Newark, DE 19702
Phone: (302) 368-5703

E-mail: info@ironhillmuseum.org
www.ironhillmuseum.org

Open: Call for days and hours; change seasonally.

Info: The Iron Hill Museum specializes in the natural history of Delaware. The rock and mineral collection includes many Delaware specimens as well as a portion of the Irenee du Pont collection, which was donated many years ago. (The remainder of this collection is at Penny Hall on the University of Delaware Campus. This display is also open to the public. See entry on University of Delaware Mineralogical Museum.)

The museum also has an excellent display of fluorescent minerals (not from Delaware). Group programs and school field trips include a walk to the old iron mines and sometimes rock collection at the top of Iron Hill and at other sites.

The Iron Mountain area was mined for iron ore for approximately 200 years. An original open-pit iron mine exists along the museum trail, as well as spoils piles resulting from mining activity.

Before iron ore was mined, large outcrops of jasper at the site brought Native Americans to the area in search of this valuable stone (lithic) resource for making the tools necessary for survival. Evidence gathered as a result of archeological excavation indicates that the site was used as both a procurement area and a workshop complex, since both finished projectile points and late-stage rejected stone material have been recovered. Jasper, along with chert and chalcedony, is restricted to a small region called the Delaware Chalcedony Complex. Iron Hill was the only jasper source in the area and was geographically the southernmost point of access for this important resource.

Admission: Call for fees.

Directions: The Iron Hill Museum is located on Old Baltimore Pike, just south of the Newark, Delaware, city limits. Call or check website for directions.

Info: For information on other Native American stone quarries, see listings in Calumet and Copper Harbor, MI: copper (Vol. 4); Pipestone, MN: pipestone quarries (Vol.1); Hopewell and Brownsville, OH: flint quarries (Vol. 4); and Fritch, TX: flint quarries (Vol. 2).

NEWARK

Museum

University of Delaware
Mineralogical Museum
Penny Hall
Academy Street
Newark, DE 19716-2544
Phone: (302) 831-8242
Fax: (302) 831-8251
www.museums.udel.edu/

Open: Closed until further notice due to scheduled renovation. Call (302) 831-8037 for information.

Info: The museum's collection includes approximately 5,000 specimens, about 1,000 of which are on display in the Irenee du Pont Memorial Room in Penny Hall. The collection of the late Irenee du Pont forms the core of the University Mineralogical Museum. Mr. du Pont had been interested in minerals for several years and in 1919 purchased the mineral collection assembled by George Kunz, which Tiffany & Co. had on display in its Fifth Avenue showroom in New York City.

Among the specimens are crystals of gem minerals. The collection has been expanded by other donors. Mrs. David Craven, a niece of Irenee du Pont, became interested in the collection and donated funds to increase the collection and expand the Mineral Room.

Admission: Free.

Directions: In Penny Hall on the university campus.

SECTION 3: Special Events and Tourist Information

TOURIST INFORMATION

State Tourist Agency

Delaware Tourism Office
99 Kings Highway
P.O. Box 1401
Wilmington, DE 19901

Phone: (302) 739-4271;
(866) 284-7483
Fax: (302) 739-5749
www.visitdelaware.net

DISTRICT OF COLUMBIA

SECTION 1: Fee Dig Sites and Guide Services

No information available.

SECTION 2: Museums and Mine Tours

Museum 🏛

Smithsonian Institution
National Museum of Natural History
10th Street and
Constitution Avenue NW
Washington, D.C. 20560-0119
Phone: (202) 633-1000
www.si.edu
(Click on "Natural History Museum," go to "Research and Collections," then go to "Mineral Sciences.")

Open: All year, 10:00 A.M.–5:30 P.M. 7 days/week. Closed December 25.
Info: Renovated in 1997, the Janet Annenberg Hooker Hall of Gems and Minerals contains nearly 3,500 gems, minerals, rocks, and meteorites from the museum's unparalleled collections. The collection includes both cut and uncut stones, including many world-famous gems. The more impressive items are housed in individual cases. The Carmen Lúcia Ruby—a 23.1-carat Burmese ruby of exceptional color and transparency—is a recent addition.

Many gems and minerals from locales listed in this book are a part of the Smithsonian collection.

The National Gem and Mineral Collection contains over 375,000 individual specimens, including the Hope Diamond and the Star of Asia Sapphire. It also contains a research mineral collection used by scientists all over the world. The National Meteorite Collection is one of the three largest meteorite collections in the world, consisting of over 4,000 specimens. The National Rock and Ore Collection contains over 235,000 specimens.
Admission: Free.
Directions: Located at the corner of 10th Street and Constitution Avenue; reachable by Metro.

SECTION 3: Special Events and Tourist Information

TOURIST INFORMATION

State Tourist Agency

Washington, D.C. Convention and
Tourism Corporation
901 7th Street NW, 4th Floor
Washington, DC 20001
Phone: (202) 789-7000
Fax: (202) 789-7037
www.washington.org

ILLINOIS

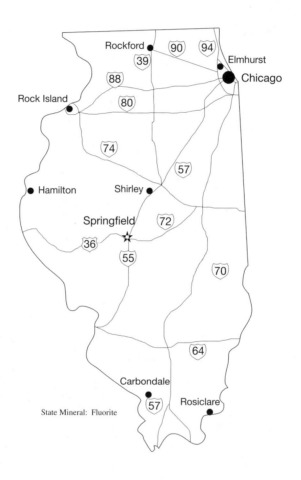

Rockford

90 94

39 Elmhurst

88 Chicago

Rock Island 80

74

57

Hamilton Shirley

Springfield 72

36

55 70

64

Carbondale

State Mineral: Fluorite 57 Rosiclare

State Mineral: Fluorite

SECTION 1: Fee Dig Sites and Guide Services

HAMILTON / *Native • Easy to Moderate*

Hunt for Geodes *T*

The following gems or minerals may be found:

- **Geodes**

Jacobs Geodes
Gary Jacobs
823 E. County Road 1220
Hamilton, IL 62341
Phone: (217) 847-3509

Open: All year, weather permitting, 8:00 A.M.–dusk.
Info: Dig geodes from a pit, or hunt them in the creek. Some have calcite, barite, quartz, or kaolinite inside; a few have water inside.
Rates: $16.00 per 5-gallon bucket.
Other services available: Mr. Jacobs has whole and cracked geodes for sale.
Directions: In Hamilton, take Highway 96S south for one mile, and look for signs for the Geode Shop and Mine.

ROSICLARE / *Native • Easy*

Dig for Fluorite in Mine Ore *T*

The following gems or minerals may be found:

- **Fluorite**

American Fluorite Museum
Main Street
P.O. Box 755
Rosiclare, IL 62982
Phone: (618) 285-3513

Open: Beginning of April–end of October; 1:00 P.M.–4:00 P.M. Thursday, Friday, Sunday; 10:00 A.M.–4:00 P.M. Saturday.
Info: Ore from the closed mine has been piled at the museum for collectors to dig for fluorite and other minerals.
Admission: Free; $1.00/pound for collected material.

SECTION 2: Museums and Mine Tours

CARBONDALE

Museum

University Museum
1000 Faner Drive, Mail Code 4508
Southern Illinois University
Carbondale, IL 62901

Phone: (618) 453-5388
E-mail: musuem@sie.edu

Open: Tuesday–Friday 10:00 A.M.–4:00 P.M., Sat.: 1:00–4:00 P.M. when school is open.
Info: Has an exhibition gallery devoted to the display of specimens representing

geologic history; their collection has over 20,000 geological specimens.

Admission: Free, donations welcome.

Directions: In the center of the university campus. Call for specific directions and for information on parking.

CHICAGO

Museum   🏛

The Field Museum
1400 S. Lake Shore Drive
Chicago, IL 60605-2496
Phone: (312) 922-9410
Fax: (312) 665-7101
www.fieldmuseum.org

Open: All year, except Christmas, 9:00 A.M.–5:00 P.M. 7 days/week. Dates of early and/or late closings are listed on the website.

Info: The gem exhibit of the Field Museum contains over 500 pieces. Displayed are the best of the Museum's 92-year-old gem collection. Most of this collection dates back to the 1893 World Exposition, when Harlow Higinbotham, a museum trustee, purchased the collection from Tiffany & Co., which had exhibited the gems during the exposition.

Visitors can learn what gems are, where they come from, and how they are used by people. Information is provided on the methods, techniques, and terminology of the gem industry, along with the superstition and lore of gemstones. The exhibit is divided into 12 sections, each

devoted to a different grouping of gems, including Quartz, Cryptocrystalline Quartz, Precious Stones, Lapidary Art, Gems from Animals and Plants, Royal Gems, Diamond Replicas, Unusual Gems, Decorative Minerals, Myth and Magic, Stars and Eyes, and What Is a Gem? The meteorite collection is world renowned.

Admission: See website or call for prices.

Directions: Roosevelt Road at Lakeshore Drive in downtown Chicago.

CHICAGO

Museum   🏛

Museum of Science and Industry
57th Street and Lake Shore Drive
Chicago, IL 60637
Phone: (773) 684-1414
E-mail: msi@msichicago.org
www.msichicago.org

Open: Monday–Saturday 9:30 A.M.–4:00 P.M., Sunday 11:00 A.M.–4:00 P.M.

Info: The museum has a tour of a simulated coal mine, Old Ben #17, which will reopen in spring 2008, after renovations.

Rates: Adults $11.00, seniors 65+ $9.50, children 3–11 $7.00, Chicago residents slightly less. Call or check the website for free admission days.

Other services available: Gift shop.

Directions: On Lake Shore Drive. Call or check the website for specific directions and information on parking.

ELMHURST

Museum 🏛

Lizzadro Museum of Lapidary Art
Wilder Park
220 Cottage Hill
Elmhurst, IL 60126
Phone: (630) 833-1616
Fax: (630) 833-1225
www.lizzadromuseum.org

Open: All year, 10:00 A.M.–5:00 P.M. Tuesday–Saturday, 1:00–5:00 P.M. Sunday. Closed Mondays and major holidays. Groups should call for reservations.

Info: Joseph F. Lizzadro, Sr., gained a first-hand appreciation for the unique characteristics of the mineral world through working with rough gem material as a hobbyist and collector. The museum opened on November 4, 1962, with this statement of purpose by the Lizzadro family: "To share with others our enjoyment of the eternal beauty in gemstones and promote the study of earth science."

The museum displays over 1,300 pieces of cut and polished gems and minerals. Displays include masterpieces of lapidary work from European countries, including Germany and Italy. Fine Chinese jadeite carvings are also displayed. Visitors can see fluorescent rocks, a birthstone display, fossils, unusual or noteworthy rocks, meteorites, and micromounts.

Admission: Adults $4.00, seniors $3.00, students and teens $2.00, children 7–12 $1.00, children under 7 free. Admission free on Fridays.

Other services available: Gift shop and educational programs on select Saturdays. Every Sunday afternoon a 50-minute video is shown which discusses how to start a mineral collection, where to search for specimens, and how to cut and polish stones.

Directions: Take St. Charles Road east from Highway 83 in Elmhurst. Turn left on Prospect to the Wilder Park entrance. An alternative route is to take York Avenue to Church Street, and turn west on Church to Prospect and turn right to Wilder Park.

ROCKFORD

Museum

Burpee Museum of Natural History
737 N. Main Street
Rockford, IL 61103
Phone: (815) 965-3433
Fax: (815) 965-2703
E-mail: info@burpee.org
www.burpee.org

Open: Monday–Saturday, 10:00 A.M.–
5:00 P.M.; Sunday, noon–5:00 P.M.

Info: Displays of rocks, minerals, gems, and exhibits on geological forces shaping our world. Extensive exhibit on local geology, updated in spring 2007.

Admission: Adults $5.00, children 3–17 $4.00. Wednesdays are free.

Other services available: Gift shop.

Directions: Located on the northern edge of downtown Rockford. Call or check the website for directions.

ROCK ISLAND

Museum

Augustana Fryxell Geology Museum
Augustana College
38th Street
Rock Island, IL 61201
Phone: (309) 794-7318
Fax: (309) 794-7564
www.augustana.edu/academ/geology

Open: During the academic school year, 8:00 A.M.–4:30 P.M. Monday–Friday;
Saturday and Sunday, 1:00 P.M.–4:00 P.M.

Info: The Fryxell Museum has become one of the largest and finest rock and mineral collections in the Midwest. All types of minerals are displayed including a fine collection of Illinois minerals as well as a state-of-the-art fluorescent display.

Admission: Free.

Directions: Located in the Swenson Hall of Geosciences on the Augustana College campus, on 38th Street in Rock Island.

ROSICLARE

Museum

The American Fluorite Museum
Main Street
P.O. Box 755
Rosiclare, IL 62982
Phone: (217) 782-7386
Fax: (217) 782-1254
http://kcminerals.com/american.htm

Open: Beginning of April–end of October, 1:00–4:00 P.M. Thursday, Friday, Sunday, 10:00 A.M.–4:00 P.M. Saturday.

Info: The museum is located in the former Rosiclare Lead and Fluorspar Mining Company office building. Displays tell the story of the fluorspar mining industry using ore specimens, mining equipment, and photographs. There is also a display of mineral specimens, including many fluorite specimens.

Admission: Adults $3.00, children 6–12 $1.00.

Directions: Call for directions.

SHIRLEY

Museum

The Funk Gem and Mineral Museum
10875 Prairie Home Lane
Shirley, IL 61772
Phone: (309) 827-6792

Open: Tours by reservation only. Tuesday–Saturday, 9:00 A.M.–4:00 P.M.

Info: The museum is located on the same site as the Prairie Home. The museum displays part of the Funk gem and mineral collection, called the biggest one-man mineral collection in the world. Displays include one gem case, 50 mineral cases with specimens from around the world (including fluorescent minerals). A petrified wood display is outside.

Admission: Free.

Directions: Call for directions when making reservations.

SPRINGFIELD

Museum

Illinois State Museum
502 S. Spring Street
Springfield, IL 62706
Phone: (217) 782-7386
Fax: (217) 782-1254
www.museum.state.il.us

Open: All year, 8:30 A.M.–5:00 P.M. 6 days/week, noon–5:00 P.M. Sunday; closed on Thanksgiving, Christmas, and New Year's Day.

Info: Rock collections at the museum contain representative samples of most rock types, including the major formations in Illinois. Touch one of the largest masses of copper, and see dioramas presenting environmental change over the last 500 million years based on geological specimens and evidence.

Admission: Free.

Other services available: Gift shop.

Directions: The museum is located on the southwest corner of the state capitol grounds, at the intersection of Spring and Edwards Streets. Free parking is available nearby.

SECTION 3: Special Events and Tourist Information

TOURIST INFORMATION

State Tourist Agency

Illinois Department of Commerce and
Economic Opportunity
100 W. Randolph Street
Suite 3–400
Chicago, IL 60601
Phone: (800) 2 CONNECT or
(800) 226-6632
E-mail: tourism@illinoisbiz.biz
www.enjoyillinois.com

INDIANA

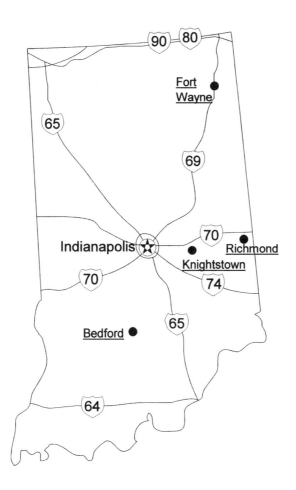

State Stone/Rock: Limestone

SECTION 1: Fee Dig Sites and Guide Services

KNIGHTSTOWN / *Native* ▪
Moderate

Midwestern
Gold Prospecting *T*

The following gems or minerals may be found:
- Gold

Yogi Bear's Jellystone Park
Camping Resort
5964 South State Road 109
Knightstown, IN 46148
Phone: (800) IGO-YOGI or
(800) 446-9644
www.jellystoneindy.com

Open: Call for hours for panning.
Info: Pan, sluice, or dredge in a creek bed, or glacial sand and gravel deposits. The resort also has special weekend events such as Old Prospectors Weekend in May and Gold Rush Weekend in September.
Fee: Free if camping. If not camping, adults $5.00, children $5.00.
Other services available: Camping cabins; fishing; camping store; showers; playground; swimming pool; paddleboats.
Directions: State Highway 109 and Interstate 70 (exit 115), 25 miles east of Indianapolis, at Knightstown.

SECTION 2: Museums and Mine Tours

BEDFORD

Museum

Land of Limestone Exhibit
Bedford Campus-Oakland City
University
405 I Street
Bedford, IN 47421
Phone: (812) 279-8126
Fax: (812) 849-0168
www.limestonecountry.com
(Click on "attractions.")

For information, write:
Lawrence County Tourism Commission

and Convention Service
533 W. Main Street
Mitchell, IN 47446
Phone: (812) 849-1090; (800) 798-0769
Fax: (812) 849-0168

Open: All year, Monday–Friday 8:00 A.M.–5:00 P.M.
Info: Limestone has been quarried in this part of southern Indiana since the mid-19th century and used to build and embellish America's most distinguished architectural landmarks, including Washington's National Cathedral, the Empire State Building, Rockefeller Center, the

United States Archives, and Grand Central Station. The Land of Limestone exhibit takes you to the sources of limestone, to the quarries and mills, and commemorates the distinguished legacy of Indiana limestone. The exhibit brings to life the people, events, and history surrounding Lawrence County's famous natural resources, Salem limestone.

Admission: Free.

Directions: Just north of the Courthouse Square Historic District.

BEDFORD

Museum

Lawrence County Museum of History
929 15th Street
Bedford, IN 47421
Phone: (812) 278-8575

Open: All year. 9:00 A.M.–4:00 P.M., Tuesday–Friday; 9:00 A.M.–3:00 P.M. Saturday.

Info: Exhibits on limestone and many other geological specimens from Lawrence County.

Directions: For more information, contact the Lawrence County Tourism Commission.

FORT WAYNE

Geosciences/Museum

Indiana Purdue University at Ft. Wayne
Fort Wayne, IN 46805

http://www.geosci.ipfw.edu

Open: 7:00 A.M.–10:00 P.M. Closed for all school breaks.

Info: Hallway displays show 285 mineral specimens, 19 meteorite specimens and 92 rock specimens. There is also a Geogarden consisting of a number of large boulder-sized local specimens on display located outside in a garden setting.

Admission: Free.

Directions: Call (260) 481-6249, or go to http://www.ipfw.edu/campus/maps/

INDIANAPOLIS

Museum

Indiana State Museum
650 W. Washington Street
Indianapolis, IN 46204
Phone: (317) 232-1637
Fax: (317) 232-7090
www.indianamuseum.org

Open: All year, 9:00 A.M.–5:00 P.M. Monday–Saturday, 11:00 A.M–5:00 P.M. Sunday. Closed major holidays.

Info: The Indiana State Museum in River State Park contains exhibits on Indiana's natural history. The building construction included Indiana stones such as limestone and sandstone.

The museum now displays mineral suites which present minerals from Indiana and the surrounding regions. Galleries tell the story of Indiana's natural history, and hands-on activities teach geologic processes. The museum's annual gem, fossil, and mineral show, GeoFest, is held in October.

Admission: Adults $7.00, seniors (above 60) $6.50, children (3–12) $4.00.

Directions: Just west of the corner of West and Washington Streets in downtown Indianapolis, in White River State Park. Parking is available in the underground garage off Washington Street.

RICHMOND

Museum

Joseph Moore Museum of Natural History
Earlham College
Drawer 68
Richmond, IN 47374
Phone: (765) 983-1303
www.earlham.edu/~muse

Open: Monday, Wednesday, and Friday 1:00 – 4:00 P.M. Sunday 1:00 – 5:00 P.M

Info: The museum was established in 1847 as a teaching collection. The geology exhibit displays geological specimens from the local Ordovician limestone.

As a college program, the museum hours reflect the academic schedule. The museum is staffed almost entirely by students, who design exhibits, maintain collections, and lead tours.

Admission: Free; donations welcome.

Directions: The museum is located on the Earlham College campus in Richmond on U.S. 40, west of the river. From I-70, take the U.S. 35 exit, drive south until you come to U.S. 40, then turn right.

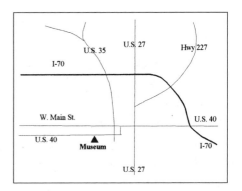

SECTION 3: Special Events and Tourist Information

TOURIST INFORMATION

State Tourist Agency

Indiana Department of Tourism Development
Indiana Tourism Division

One North Capitol, Suite 600
Indianapolis, IN 46204-2288
Phone: (800) 677-9800
Fax: (317) 233-6887
www.enjoyindiana.com

MAINE

Caribou
Presque Isle

95

Auburn
Bethel
West Paris 495
Poland
Portland
Augusta
ACADIA
NATIONAL PARK

State Mineral: Tourmaline (1971)

The Story of Maine Tourmaline

A band of mineralization runs from the Maine coast at Brunswick through Auburn and Newry and into New Hampshire. In this area or band are found Maine tourmaline and other gems and minerals. This band of mineralization was formed 300 million years ago when intense volcanic activity resulted in lava flowing into cracks in the existing granite rock. As the lava and surrounding rock cooled, gems and mineral crystals formed in voids in the rock. Over the intervening time, rain and glaciers have eroded the overlying rock, bringing the crystal-bearing voids near or to the surface. In some instances, the rock was so eroded that the crystals were released into the soil and washed down the slope. Thus, the crystals are found in both soil and rock.

Maine tourmaline was first discovered in 1820 by two students who spent much of their leisure time hunting gems in the area around Paris, Maine. Late that year, while exploring Mt. Mica, one of the students found an intense green crystal—a tourmaline—in the soil. When the students returned the next spring, they found more crystals and crystal fragments. Crystals were found in a multitude of colors, including green, red, yellow, and white. Tourmaline has been mined from Mt. Mica for over 175 years; major finds are still being made. A crystal found in 1978 yielded several cut gems, including a blue-green 256-carat stone.

Other major finds have also been made in this band of mineralization. Tourmaline has been found on Mt. Apatite, in Auburn, since 1839, and tourmaline has been mined there sporadically since 1883. The Plumbago Mining Company was established in 1972 following the discovery of tourmaline on Plumbago Mountain. In the following year and a half, over 1 metric ton of tourmaline, much of it gem quality, was recovered.

One unique type of tourmaline found in Maine is watermelon tourmaline, which has a deep red center and a green outer layer. Another type of tourmaline found in Maine, but in few other locations, is bicolor tourmaline, in which the crystals have one color at one end and a different color at the other. A few tricolor crystals have even been found. Most of the quarries are closed or private, but some collecting can be done.

(Portions of this text are excerpted from "The History of Maine Tourmaline" with permission from Cross Jewelers, Portland, ME.)

AUBURN / *Native* ▪ *Moderate*

Hunt for Gems and Minerals *T*

The following gems and minerals may be found:

▪ Apatite, tourmaline, quartz

City of Auburn/Feldspar and
Greenlaw Quarries
48 Pettengill Park
Auburn, ME 04210
Phone: (207) 333-6000
Fax: (207) 784-0192

Open: Dawn–dusk. Dept. office hours: open Monday–Friday 8:00 A.M.–4:30 P.M.

Info: Rock hunting and mining has occurred in the park area for over 150 years. There are specific rules and guidelines for collecting in the park; contact the city offices.

Directions: Call for directions.

AUBURN / *Native* ▪ *Moderate*

Hunt for Gems and Minerals *T*

The following gems and minerals may be found:

▪ Tourmaline, black tourmaline, garnet, graphic granite, clevelandite, autenite, mica, beryl

Mt. Apatite Farm/Turner Quarry
171 Hatch Road
Auburn, ME 04210

Phone: (207) 795-6376; (207) 650-1573
E-mail: cookincarol@maine.com
www.cookincarol.com

Open: May–October; call for hours and reservations.

Info: This is one of several old feldspar and gem quarries on Mt. Apatite. The farm is a catering business; however, the owner allows collecting in the quarry.

Admission: Adults $5.00, under 18 free.

Directions: Get directions when you make a reservation.

BETHEL / *Native* ▪ *Moderate*

Collect Your Own Gems and Minerals *T*

The following gems and minerals may be found:

▪ Albite, almandine garnet, beryl, rose and other varieties of quartz, black tourmaline, biotite, autunite, zircon

Maine Mineralogy Expeditions
The Bumpus Quarry
121 Mayville Road
Bethel, ME 04217
Phone: (207) 824-4224;
(800) 533-3607
Fax: (207) 824-8511
E-mail: info@betheloutdooradventure.com
www.rocksme.biz

Open: May–October, by reservation.

Info: Two different methods of collecting

are available. Tailngs from the Bumpus Mine have been transported to the Bethel Outdoor Adventures campground, where a sluice has been set up. Pails of gem dirt can be purchased and sluiced; keep everything you find.

Several times a month educational/collecting tours leave from the campground and go to the Bumpus Mine, a feldspar mine which was closed sometime in the 1950s or 1960s. After a presentation and tour of the quarry and mine tunnels, you can dig in the tailing and in some parts of the mine.

Admission: Call for prices.

BETHEL / *Native • Moderate to Difficult*

Collect Minerals at a Working Aquamarine Mine *T*

The following gems or minerals may be found (these have been observed to date):

• Beryl (aquamarine variety), quartz (smoky and milky), albite feldspar, black tourmaline, garnet, mica, pyrite, amethyst (rare), zircon, biotite mica, hydroxyl herderite, columbite, rutile, apatite, siderite, and hyalite opal

Songo Pond Mine
Jan Neal Brownstein
40 South Shore Lane
P.O. Box 864
Bethel, ME 04217
Phone: (207) 824-3898

Open: Late spring until snow (November)

8:00 A.M.– 4:00 P.M. Daily admissions are limited. Call ahead—advance reservations required.

Site may be closed to visitors during certain mining operations or inclement weather.

Info: The mine is open to the public on a seasonal basis and gives a chance to collect minerals from the mine tailings (dump area) and observe a small-scale mining operation at the same time. Bring your own equipment (hammer, chisel, scraper, shovel, screen, etc.). Boots, safety glasses, gloves, and hats are recommended for protective clothing, along with sunscreen. Also, bring something to drink and whatever you will need to eat.

Admission: Adults full day $25.00, up to 4 hours $15.00; children under 12 full day $7.50, 4 hour pass $5.00; children under 6 free. Collection limit: one 5-gallon pail. Groups call ahead for a discount.

Other services available: New shop 800 feet from mine sells jewelry, gemstones, and mineral specimens. Gem cutting will be available. Tools also for sale. A portable toilet is provided at the mine.

Directions: From Route 26 or Route 2, travel to the town of Bethel; you will see a sign for Route 5 south. Travel 4 miles south to the south shore of Songo Pond, then look for a highway sign for South Shore Lane, which is a dirt road on the left. Take South Shore Lane, and the mine parking lot is ¼ mile on the right.

The parking lot is a 5–10-minute

walk from the mine. Handicapped and elderly persons may use limited parking at the top of the hill, 150 feet from the mine. Others may drive up and leave passengers and tools at the mine, then drive back down to the parking lot at the bottom.

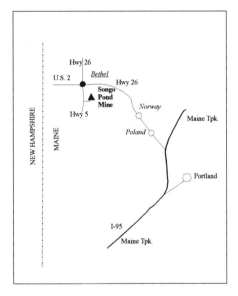

POLAND / *Native ▪ Moderate to Difficult*

Camp and Collect Minerals in Maine 𝑇

The following gems or minerals may be found:

▪ Tourmaline, beryl, garnet, mica, quartz, albite, columbite, rutile, apatite, and other Maine gems and minerals (See complete list on page 64)

Poland Mining Camps
Mary Groves
P.O. Box 26
Poland, ME 04274
Phone: (207) 998-2350
www.polandminingcamps.com

Open: June 1–September 30 by reservation only.

Info: Check the website for upcoming special events. Collect minerals at pegmatite quarries closed to the public. Poland Mining Camps have collection access at Mount Mica Quarry, Emmons Quarry, Mount Apatite, Pulsifer Quarry, Keith Quarry, Wade Quarry, Hole-in-the-Ground Quarry, Dionne Quarry, Marie Luise Hopfe Quarry, Newry Mine, G. E. Mine, and others.

This is a unique vacation opportunity. Fee includes lodging, all meals, mine fees, and a guide to famous and active quarries. Lodging is in cabins with two private bedrooms, living room with fireplace (only heat for the cabin), ½ kitchen with fridge, etc., and bath with flush facilities and shower (hot and cold). All linens, bedding, and towels are provided. At the center of the camp complex is a pavilion, which is the hub of activity at the camp. It is used for meals, functions, and general socializing with other campers. Minerals are displayed from the various quarries where you hunt for gems, and lectures and demonstrations by local craftsmen and miners are presented there.

Minerals List
(Some of the More Common Minerals That May Be Found)

Apatite (fluor-)
Apatite (hydroxyl-)
Albite
Albite (cleavelandite var.)
Almandine garnet
Arsenopyrite
Autenite
Beryl (aquamarine, morganite, goshenite)
Beryllonite
Bertrandite
Biotite mica

Casserite
Columbite
Gahnite (spinel)
Hydroxyl-Herderite
Kaolinite
Lepidolite mica
Lithiophillite
Lollingite
Microcline/orthoclase (feldspar)
Montebrasite
Montmorillonite
Muscovite mica

Petalite
Pollucite
Pyrite
Quartz
Rhodochrosite
Spodumene
Topaz
Tourmaline (elbaite)
Tourmaline (schorl)
Triphyllite
Uranite
Zircon

Phosphate Species Minerals
(That May Be Found in Addition to the Ones Listed Above)

Augelite
Beraumite
Bermanite
Brazilianite
Childrenite
Diadochite
Dickinsonite
Earlshannonite
Eosphorite
Farifieldite
Gainsite
Goyazite
Graftonite
Heterosite

Hureaylite
Jahnsite
Kosnarite
Landsite
Laueite
Ludlamite
McCrillisite
Mitridatite
Monzaite
Moraesite
Perhamite
Phosphosiderite
Phosphouranylite
Purpurite

Reddingite
Rochbridgeite
Stewartite
Strunzite
Switzerite (and metaswitzerite)
Torberite
Triplite
Uralolite
Vivianite
Wardite
Whitlockite
Whitmoreite
Wodginite

The late Dudy Groves had over 30 years of experience in mining and collecting gemstones and minerals in the local quarries. He worked for and/or mined in many of the historically important mining operations, including Mount Apatite and Mount Mica. Mary Groves is in charge of the large organic garden, which supplies much of the food for the camp. She is famous for her down-home cooking and will cater to any special dietary needs. Mary is continuing mining at Mt. Apatite with the help of many wonderful people.

Fee: $600.00 per person per week for cabins, $125.00 per person per day for a 3-day stay (minimum length of stay). Must provide your own equipment, protective clothing, and transportation. Reservations and a nonrefundable 50% deposit required. Walk-ins will be accommodated only if space is available.

Serious mineral collectors who can't stay at Poland Mining Camps may still join the resident clients on selected days and collect at the Quarry-of-the-Day, selected by Poland Mining Camps. The Tag-a-long Package includes quarry access, quarry fees, up to 7 hours of collecting time (dependent on travel times and other variables), liability coverage, and the services of the guide. It does not include food, lodging, transportation, or other services of the Camps. With the Tag-a-long Package, which requires a reservation, you must join the caravan leaving Poland Mining Camps at 8:00 A.M. and leave the quarry when the guide leaves. Tag-a-long customers must follow all rules and restrictions of Poland Mining Camps and must stay with and follow directions of the Poland Mining Camps guide. You may not enter or return to the Quarry-of-the-Day on your own at any time.

Tag-a-Long Rates: $60.00 per person per day; 10% discount for 3 consecutive days. Prices subject to change.

Note: All prices are subject to change and to sales tax.

Directions: From I-95 take exit 63, Gray. Go north on Route 26 to Poland. Continue north for a couple of miles. Poland Mining Camps is on the right, just before the junction of Route 26 and Route 11.

WEST PARIS / *Native • Moderate to Difficult*

Collect Minerals in Maine

The following gems or minerals may be found:

- Tourmaline (including green and black); beryl; scheelite; quartz crystals; albite; columbite; apatite; amethyst; spodumene; zircon; petalite; cookeite; and other Maine gems and minerals

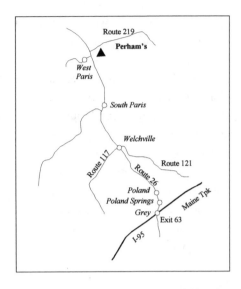

Perham's of West Paris
P.O. Box 280
West Paris, ME 04289
Phone: (207) 674-2341; (800) 371-GEMS or (800) 371-4367
Fax: (207) 674-3692

Open: Shop open all year, May–December 9:00 A.M.– 5:00 P.M., 7 days/week; January–April, closed Mondays and Tuesdays, 9:00 A.M.–4:00 P.M., Wednesday–Sunday. Sites may be closed to visitors during occasional mining operations; closed Thanksgiving and Christmas.

Info: Perham's owns five quarries located within 10 miles of the shop. Information on these quarries is found on the next page. Maps are available free at the shop. Before going to the quarries, you may study the museum displays to learn to recognize minerals that can be found locally. Bring your own equipment and protective clothing. Keep what you find in your collecting venture.

Rates: May visit quarries free of charge.

Other services available: Shop sells fine jewelry, gemstones and mineral specimens, also prospecting tools, books, and gifts. Museum (for further information, see listing in Section 2).

Directions: Take exit 63 on the Maine Turnpike; then Maine Route 26 north to West Paris, and Perham's.

Important Note: During late October and November, hunting season is open. The land owned by Perham's is *not* posted, so it is advisable to wear blaze orange when visiting the quarries during this time.

Perham's Quarries

Local quarries are all open pits, and collecting usually takes place in the surrounding dump areas, or tailings. Actual mining is sporadic, but mineral collecting is an ongoing activity taking place when weather permits. Common-sense safety guidelines offer adequate protection. What you find will depend upon your persistence—and your luck.

Harvard Quarry

This renowned locale was initially developed about 1870 by George "Shavey" Noyes. Harvard University conducted a mining operation here in 1917, and the quarry was mined by Arthur Valley in 1942. Since 1958 this locale, owned by the Perham family, has been explored sporadically by Frank Perham. The Harvard is noted for fine crystals of purple apatite as well as for green tourmaline, black tourmaline, garnet, beryl, quartz, and cookeite. Amethyst, cassiterite, zircon, petalite, columbite, gahnite, spodumene, scheelite, vesuvianite, and lepidolite are also found here.

Tamminen Quarry

Mining here began about 1930, and the quarry has since been explored by several mining firms. Owned by Nestor Tamminen for many years, this site was a valued source of feldspar. Among the minerals found here are amblygonite, pollucite, cleavelandite, montmorillonite, and altered spodumene. This locale is renowned for especially fine pseudocubic quartz crystals.

Waisanen Quarry

Mining here began in 1931 when Matti Waisanen conducted an exploration directed at the recovery of mica. The quarry has since been mined extensively for mica and feldspar, both commercially valuable materials. Frank Perham's 1963 mining endeavor produced superb specimens of hydroxyl-herderite, bertrandite, purple apatite, and superb parallel-growth quartz crystals. Other mineral varieties found here include gem tourmaline, spodumene, triphylite, and columbite.

SECTION 2: Museums and Mine Tours

AUGUSTA

Museum

Maine State Museum
83 State House Station
Augusta, ME 04333-0083
Phone: (207) 287-2301
Fax: (207) 287-6633
www.maine.gov/museum/

Open: All year; closed major holidays. 9:00 A.M.–5:00 P.M. Monday–Friday, 10:00 A.M.–4:00 P.M. Saturday, 1:00–4:00 P.M. Sunday.

Info: Gem and mineral cases present a display of Maine gemstones, including smoky quartz, milky quartz, rose quartz, amethyst, garnet, beryl, and gold. Various types of the Maine state mineral, tourmaline, are on display. The Peary necklace, which Arctic explorer Robert Peary gave to his wife for a birthday present in 1913, is on display. It is made from gold collected from the Swift River in western Maine, and Maine tourmaline.

Admission: Adults, $2.00; seniors, $1.00; students ages 6–18, $1.00; children under 6, free. $6.00 maximum/family.

Directions: Take Interstate I-95, exit 109 to route 202 (Western Avenue). Take Western Avenue to rotary. At the rotary take RT 201 South (State Street). The state capitol will be on your right. The museum is located past the capitol on your right.

BETHEL

Museum

Maine Mineral Museum
Mt. Mann Jeweler's Gallery
57 Main Street
Bethel, ME 04217
Phone: (207) 824-3030
mtmann@megalink.net
www.mtmann.com

Open: Monday–Friday, 9:00 A.M.–5:00 P.M.; Saturday, 10:00 A.M.–5:00 P.M.

Info: Tour the Maine Mineral Museum

and the Crystal Cave for Kids. The museum presents examples of gems from both local and world-wide sources. The Crystal Cave provides kids an opportunity to see and collect local minerals in the rough.

Admission: Free.

Directions: On Main Street in Bethel.

CARIBOU

Museum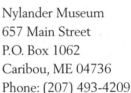

Nylander Museum
657 Main Street
P.O. Box 1062
Caribou, ME 04736
Phone: (207) 493-4209
E-mail: nylander@mfx.net
www.nylandermuseum.org

Open: May 28–Labor Day, Tuesday–Saturday, 12:30 P.M.–4:30 P.M.; Labor Day–May 28, Tuesday–Thursday, 3:00 P.M.–7:00 P.M. closed holidays. Open other times by appointment.

Info: Contains a collection of minerals from northern Maine.

Admission: Free, donations appreciated.

Directions: On Main Street in Caribou.

PRESQUE ISLE

Museum

The Northern Maine Museum of Science
Folsom Hall
University of Maine at Presque Isle

181 Main Street
Presque Isle, ME 04769
Phone: (207) 768-9400
www.umpi.maine.edu/info/nmms/
museum.htm

Open: When the campus is open. Check website for details.

Info: This museum formally opened in 1996, and contains displays in hallways on several floors, and in the entrances to Folsom Hall. Displays include minerals of Maine, Earth history, Tourmaline, Maine slate, fluorescent minerals, and crystals and their atomic structure.

Admission: Free

Directions: On the University of Maine campus at Presque Isle. Call for specific directions.

WEST PARIS

Museum

Perham's of West Paris
Route 26
P.O. Box 280
West Paris, ME 04289
Phone: (207) 674-2341;
(800) 371-GEMS or (800) 371-4367
Fax: (207) 674-3692

Open: Shop open all year, May–December 9:00 A.M.– 5:00 P.M. 7 days/week; January 1–April 1, 9:00 A.M.–4:00 P.M.,

closed Mondays and Tuesdays; closed Thanksgiving and Christmas.

Info: Stanley Perham started in the gemstone business in 1919, and the family-owned business has grown since that time. *Museum Attractions Include:*
▪ Collection of Maine minerals and gems
▪ Model of a working feldspar quarry
▪ The MERCROPON gem cutting developed by Stanley Perham and other local men interested in gem cutting, which served as a prototype for the development of modern faceting machines
▪ A model of a gem tourmaline pocket
▪ A collection of fluorescent minerals

Admission: Free.

Directions: Take exit 11 on the Maine Turnpike; then Maine Route 26 north to West Paris, and Perham's.

ANNUAL EVENT

Maine Mineral Symposium, Augusta, Maine

The symposium includes lectures, exhibits, displays, and dealers. Several mineral localities are available for field collecting. Held second full weekend (Friday–Sunday) in May.

For registration or more information on the symposium, visit:
www.maine.gov
(In the "Search maine.gov" box, enter Maine Mineral Symposium.)

ANNUAL EVENT

Maine Pegmatite Workshop, Poland, Maine

One week at the end of May or beginning of June, held at Poland Mining Camp. A Saturday–Friday program, generally with classroom activities in the morning and field trips in the afternoon. Includes a textbook on pegmatites and a faculty ranging from college professors to local miners.

For more information contact:
Raymond Sprague
93 Main Street, #9
Andover, MA 01810
Phone: (978) 475-8435
E-mail: rasprague@mac.com

TOURIST INFORMATION

State Tourist Agency

Maine Office of Tourism
#59 State House Station
Augusta, ME 04333-0059
Phone: (888) 624-6345
www.visitmaine.com

MARYLAND

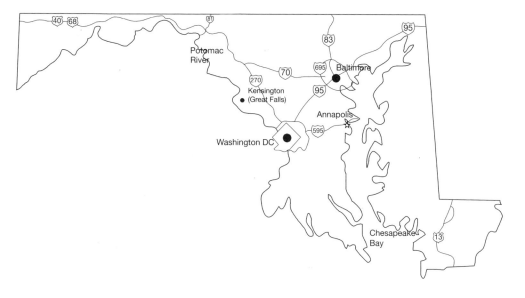

State Mineral: Patuxent River Stone

SECTION 1: Fee Dig Sites and Guide Services

No information available.

SECTION 2: Museums and Mine Tours

KENSINGTON

Gold Mine Trail

Great Falls Tavern Visitor's Center
C&O Canal National Historical Park
Kensington, MD 20891
Phone: (301) 767-3714
www.nps.gov/choh/recreation/trails/
gold.html

Open: During daylight hours.
Info: This is a 2-hour hike that goes past old gold mine workings in the Great Falls National Park. Guided tours are scheduled only periodically. Call for information.

Admission: Park entrance fee is $4.00.
Other services available: Geology hikes are also conducted periodically.
Directions: I-495 to the Cabin John Parkway west. Turn left at the intersection with MacArthur Boulevard, and continue 2.2 miles to the park entrance. Turn left into the park, continue to the admission booth, then to the Great Falls Tavern Visitor's Center.

SECTION 3: Special Events and Tourist Information

TOURIST INFORMATION

State Tourist Agency

Maryland Office of Tourism
217 E. Redwood Street
Baltimore, MD 21202
Phone: (866) 639-3526 or
(800) 719-5900; (866) MDWELCOME
www.visitmaryland.org

MASSACHUSETTS

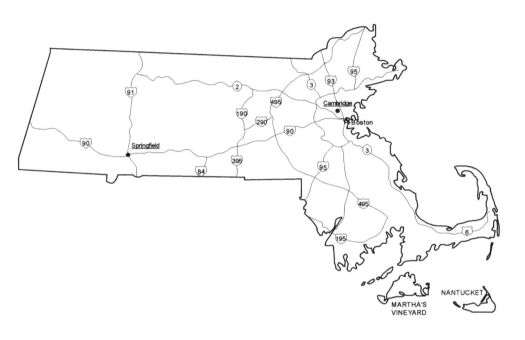

State Gemstone: Rhodonite
State Mineral: Babingtonite
State Stone/Rock: Plymouth Rock; Dighton Rock;
Roxbury Conglomerate

SECTION 1: Fee Dig Sites and Guide Services

No information available.

SECTION 2: Museums and Mine Tours

CAMBRIDGE

Museum

Harvard Museum of Natural History
Harvard University
26 Oxford Street
Cambridge, MA 02138
Phone: (617) 495-3045
www.hmnh.harvard.edu/

Open: All year, 9:00 A.M.–5:00 P.M. daily. Closed major holidays.

Info: The exhibits feature a comprehensive collection of gems, minerals, ores, and meteorites. Begun in 1784, the museum's collections cover virtually the entire scope of the mineral sciences, with 50,000 specimens.

The petrology collection and economic geology collection, comprising suites of igneous, sedimentary, and metamorphic rocks and ores (75,000+ specimens), are an impressive sampling of the Earth's crust.

Meteorites provide insight into the origin of the solar system and the universe. In 1883 the museum augmented its holdings by the acquisition of the J.

Lawrence Smith Collection. The museum has a broadly representative collection of over 514 meteorites, some of which are on display.

The museum also has an exhibit on New England gems and minerals.

Admission: Adults $9.00, non-Harvard students with ID and seniors $7.00, children 3–18 $6.00. Group rates available. Free entry Sunday 9:00 A.M.–noon.

Directions: From Storrow Drive, exit at Harvard Square/Cambridge. Proceed across the Charles River, straight through the traffic lights at Memorial Drive onto JFK Street, then continue straight through the next two traffic lights. At the third light, go straight, and veer slightly left past the subway "T" station and "Out of Town News." At the next fork in the road, stay to the left and then get immediately into the right lane, which leads to Massachusetts Avenue heading north. Continue on Massachusetts Avenue for 0.2 miles, then turn right onto Everett Street. At the next set of traffic lights, turn right onto Oxford Street. The museum is on the left, at 26 Oxford Street.

Note: Street parking is very limited. University-owned lots require a pre-paid day permit which can be obtained through a link on the museum website.

SPRINGFIELD

Museum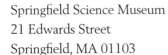

Springfield Science Museum
21 Edwards Street
Springfield, MA 01103

Phone: (413) 263-6800;
(800) 625-7738
www.springfieldmuseums.org/
museums/science/

Open: All year, 10:00 A.M.–5:00 P.M. Tuesday–Saturday; 11:00 A.M.–5:00 P.M. Sunday.

Info: Mineral Hall displays minerals from around the world, including a collection made by two local jewelers. It also has a fluorescent mineral display, specimens of local minerals, and a meteorite from Arizona.

Admission: Adults $10.00, seniors $7.00, college students $7.00, children (3–17) $5.00, children under 3 free.

Directions: The museum is located on 21 Edwards Street. Free parking is available in the Springfield Library and Museum lot on Edwards Street and on State Street directly across from the library.

SECTION 3: Special Events and Tourist Information

TOURIST INFORMATION

State Tourist Agency

Massachusetts Office of Travel and Tourism
10 Park Plaza, Suite 4510
Boston, MA 02116

Phone: (617) 973-8500;
(800) 227-MASS or (800) 227-6277
Fax: (617) 973-8525
E-mail: vacationinfo@state.ma.us
www.mass-vacation.com

MICHIGAN

State Gemstone: Isle Royal Greenstone (Chlorostrolite) (1965)
State Stone/Rock: Petosky Stone (1965)

GRAND MARAIS / *Native • Easy*

Collect Agates along the Beach *T*

The following gems or minerals may be found:

▪ Agates

Woodland Park Campground
P.O. Box 430
Grand Marais, MI 49839
Park phone: (906) 494-2613
Office phone: (906) 494-2381
www.grandmaraismichigan.com/
WoodlandPark/html

Open: April–October.

Info: This is a campground on the shores of Lake Superior; the beach is accessible for agate collecting.

Rates: Call or check the website for rates. Full hook up or primitive sites are available. First come, first served basis; reservations are not accepted.

Other services available: Camping, recreational facilities.

Directions: On Brazel Street in Grand Marais. Call for directions.

MOHAWK / *Native • Easy*

Find Your Own Copper *T*

The following gems or minerals may be found:

▪ Copper

Delaware Copper Mine
HCI, Box 102
Mohawk, MI 49950
Phone: (906) 289-4688
www.uptravel.com/attractions/
copmine.htm

Open: Seven days a week. 10:00 A.M.–6:00 P.M. June, July, August; 10:00 A.M.–5:00 P.M. September–October.

Info: Search for souvenir copper at an authentic copper mine dating back to 1847–1887.

Admission: For further information on the mine tour, see listing under Section 2.

Directions: Located in the historic ghost town of Delaware, 12 miles south of Copper Harbor and 38 miles north of Houghton on U.S. 41.

ONTONAGON / *Native • Easy*

Collect Your Own Copper and Minerals *T*

The following gems or minerals may be found:

- Native pure copper, silver, epidote, calcite, datolite, quartz

The Caledonia Copper Mine
Red Metal Minerals
202 Ontonagon Street
Ontonagon, MI 49953
Phone: (906) 884-6618
Fax: (906) 884-6753

E-mail: caledoniamine@charter.net
www.caledoniamine.com

Open: Collecting by reservation only.
Info: As seen on Travel Channel's *Cash and Treasures* program. Collect in your own ore pile on the surface and go underground to see how mining is done. An educational experience for the entire family.
Rates: Call or e-mail for information.
Directions: The mine is located about 14 miles from Ontonagon, MI, 41 miles from Houghton, and 62 miles from Ironwood. Get specific directions when you make a reservation.

SECTION 2: Museums and Mine Tours

ANN ARBOR

Museum 🏛

Exhibit Museum of Natural History
University of Michigan
1109 Geddes Avenue
Ann Arbor, MI 48019-1079
Phone: (734) 764-0478
Fax: (734) 647-2767
www.exhibits.lsa.umich.edu/
exhibitmuseum

Open: All year, 9:00 A.M.–5:00 P.M. Monday–Saturday, noon–5:00 P.M. Sunday. Closed major holidays.
Info: The museum has geology displays of rocks and minerals.
Admission: Free.

Directions: On Geddes Avenue at Washtenaw Avenue in Ann Arbor.

BLOOMFIELD HILLS

Museum 🏛

Cranbrook Institute of Science
39221 Woodward Avenue
Bloomfield Hills, MI 48303-0801
Phone: (248) 645-3200
http://science.cranbrook.edu/

Open: All year, 10:00 A.M.–5:00 P.M. Saturday–Thursday, 10:00 A.M.–10:00 P.M. Friday.
Info: Mineral Hall contains numerous cases displaying approximately 5,000 minerals from all over the world. This prize

collection of minerals and crystals includes what has been described as an almost perfect hiddenite crystal and what is perhaps the finest gold specimen in the world.

Admission: Adults $8.00, children 2–12 and seniors $6.00, children under 2 free.

Directions: Located at 39221 Woodward Avenue in Bloomfield Hills. Cranbrook is located on the west side of Woodward Avenue between Long Lake and Lone Pine Roads. From I-75, exit Big Beaver (west) to Woodward Avenue (north). From I-696; exit Woodward Avenue (north). From Telegraph: Long Lake Road (east) to Woodward Avenue (south).

CALUMET

Mining Museum

Summer:
Coppertown, U.S.A.
Red Jacket Road
Calumet, MI 49913
Phone: (906) 337-4354
www.uppermichigan.com/coppertown

Off-season:
Coppertown, U.S.A.
1197 Calumet Avenue
Calumet, MI 49913
Phone: (800) 338-7982

Open: June–mid-October, 10:00 A.M.–5:00 P.M. Monday–Saturday. Sunday (July–August) 12:30 P.M.– 4:00 P.M.

Info: The mining museum is an introduction to the story of the copper country and Keweenaw Peninsula, and America's first real mining boom. Michigan's copper industry began thousands of years ago when ancient miners attacked exposed veins of pure copper with huge hammer-stones. The tools and techniques of mining advanced considerably in the centuries that followed, and Coppertown's mining museum traces this evolution of mines and mining people with a series of exhibits designed for the family visitor.

Admission: Adults $3.00, children 12–18 $1.00, National Park Pass $2.00, children under 12 free.

Other services: Gift shop.

Directions: Turn west off U.S. 41 (Calumet Avenue) onto Red Jacket Road, and travel 1½ blocks to the museum on the left.

For information on other Native American stone quarries, see listings in Newark, DE: jasper quarries (Vol. 4); Copper Harbor, MI: copper (Vol. 4); Pipestone, MN: pipestone quarries (Vol.1); Hopewell, OH: flint quarries (Vol. 4); and Fritch, TX: flint quarries (Vol. 2).

CASPIAN

Museum

Iron County Museum and Park
P.O. Box 272
Caspian, MI 49915
Phone: (906) 265-2617
www.ironcountymuseum.com

Open: May: weekdays 8:30 A.M.–2:00 P.M.; June, July, August: Monday–Saturday 9:00 A.M.–5:00 P.M., Sunday 1:00–5:00 P.M.; September: Monday–Saturday 10:00 A.M.–4:00 P.M., Sunday 1:00 P.M.–4:00 P.M. Off-months and special times by appointment. *Note:* Times may change in May so call ahead.

Info: Sample over 110 years of history at a park and museum with 21 buildings moved to the site of the head frame and engine house of the Caspian Mine. This mine was originally opened in 1903, and shipped over 6.6 million tons of iron ore before it was shut down in 1937. Besides the head frame and engine house (on the National Registry of Historic Places), the park contains a diamond drill rig (reported to be one of only three existing in the world), a simulated scraper drift, a mine ore rail car, and two mining halls containing artifacts, displays, and models telling the story of iron ore mining in Michigan over the last century.

Admission: Call for rates.

Other services available: Gift shop.

Directions: Brady at Museum Road in Caspian, off M-189, or 2 miles off U.S. 2 at Iron River.

CHELSEA

Discovery Center

Gerald E. Eddy Discovery Center
Waterloo Recreation Area
17030 Bush Road
Chelsea, MI 48118
Phone: (734) 475-3170

Open: January–Easter Sunday, Tuesday–Saturday, 10:00 A.M.–5:00 P.M.; Sunday after Easter until Thanksgiving, Tuesday–Saturday, 10:00 A.M.–5:00 P.M., Sunday noon–5:00 P.M. Closed Thanksgiving Day through December. Closed state holidays and Mondays but open Memorial Day, July 4th, and Labor Day.

Info: The center introduces the world of geology with a focus on Michigan rocks, minerals, crystals, and mining from prehistoric times through the 20th century. Visitors can see displays, exhibits, and a multiprojector slide show. There is also an easy geology walking trail, ⅛ mile long.

Admission: A State Park Vehicle pass is required to enter all Michigan State Parks—cost $6.00/day resident, $8.00 non-resident, $24.00/year resident, $29.00/year non-resident. No charge to enter the Discovery Center.

Other services available: Gift shop.

The center is part of the 20,000-acre Waterloo Recreation Area, which features four campgrounds, a swimming beach, picnic sites, hiking, skiing, and horse trails.

Directions: From I-94, take exit 157, then take Pierce Road north to Bush

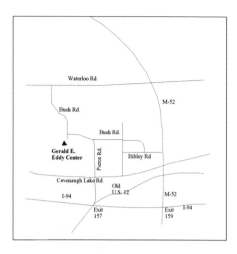

Road. When Pierce Road ends, turn left to Bush Road, then left again to the Discovery Center.

COPPER HARBOR

Mine Tour

Fort Wilkins Historic State Park
P.O. Box 71
Copper Harbor, MI 49918
Phone: (906) 289-4215
www.michigan.gov/ftwilkins

Open: Early-May–early-October, daily 8:00 A.M.–dusk.

Info: The interpretation of copper mining in the Copper Harbor region between 1840 and 1860 takes place in three locations at the State Park. One is within the fort, showing all phases of mining, beginning with the initial discovery and including Native American artifacts. A map shows the underlying geography and location of several old mine shafts. An interpretive walking trail at the lighthouse complex takes the visitor to the still-visible remains of a copper silicate vein (which gave Copper Harbor its name) and to the site of the first commercial copper mine in Michigan. Finally, there are several other mining pits located within the grounds of the fort, some of which have interpretive information.

Admission: A State Park Vehicle pass is required to enter all Michigan State Parks—cost varies. Michigan residents $6.00/day, $24.00/year; non-residents $8.00/day, $29.00/year.

Directions: Take U.S. 45 north from the Michigan-Wisconsin border to State Highway 26. Take Highway 26 north to Copper Harbor.

For information on other Native American stone quarries, see listings in Newark, DE: jasper quarries (Vol. 4); Calumet, MI: copper (Vol. 4); Pipestone, MN: pipestone quarries (Vol.1); Hopewell, OH: flint quarries (Vol. 4); and Fritch, TX: flint quarries (Vol. 2).

GREENLAND

Mine Tour 🏛

Adventure Copper Mine
Matthew & Victoria Portfleet
Greenland, MI 49929
Phone: (906) 883-3371
E-mail: mportfleet@yahoo.com
www.ontonagon.net/adventuremine/

Open: Late May to October; 9:00 A.M.–6:00 P.M. daily, 11:00 A.M.–6:00 P.M. Sunday. After Labor Day closed Wednesdays.

Info: Take a guided tour of an underground copper mine. Tours range from a historic surface tour to an underground walking tour, and even an underground cliff climb to lower mine levels. See website for age limitations and safety discussions.

Admission:
- Surface tour or trammer tour—adults $11.00, children 6–12 $6.50, under 6 free.
- Surface plus trammer—adults $17.50, children 6–12 $9.50.
- Prospector's underground tour—adults $23.50, children $15.50.
- Miners underground tour—adults $55.00.

Other services available: Hiking trails, gift shop.

Directions: Off M-28, 12 miles east of Ontonagon. Call for directions or see website.

HANCOCK

Museum/Mine Tour

The Quincy Mine Hoist Association
49750 U.S. Highway 41
Hancock, MI 49930
Phone: (906) 482-3101
Fax: (906) 482-5569
www.quincymine.com

Open: 8:30 A.M.–7:00 P.M. Monday–Saturday, 12:30 P.M.–7:00 P.M. Sunday; spring and fall, limited hours, call ahead.

Info: First-hand glimpse of what our nation's first mineral boom was like. Visitors will experience a total copper mining experience, including visits to the steam hoist buildings, the Number Two Shafthouse, and the underground copper mine. The Quincy Steam Hoist is the world's largest steam-driven hoist and was first operational in 1920. The underground mine tour includes the East Adit and the experimental mine run by the Michigan Technological University.

Admission: Full mine tour and surface tour, adults (13–54) $15.00, seniors $14.00, youth (6–12) $12.00, children under 5 free. Surface mine tour and train ride, adults and seniors $12.00, children 6–13 $5.00. AAA discount available.

Other services available: Gift shop.

Directions: Located on Route U.S. 41 North in Hancock.

HOUGHTON

Museum 🏛

The A. E. Seaman Mineral Museum
Michigan Technological University
1400 Townsend Drive
Houghton, MI 49931-1295
Phone: (906) 487-2572
Fax: (906) 487-3027
www.museum.mtu.edu

Open: All year, 9:00 A.M.–4:30 P.M. Monday–Friday, noon–5:00 P.M. Saturday and Sunday (July–September). Closed on university holidays. Group tours by prior arrangement.

Info: Michigan Technological University's A. E. Seaman Mineral Museum (SMM), one of the best U.S. mineral museums, is recognized worldwide for having one of the premier natural crystal collections in North America. Founded in 1902 by pioneer Lake Superior geologist Arthur Edmund Seaman, the SMM collection today totals more than 30,000 mineral specimens, of which some 5,000 are currently on exhibit. The museum's collections include an irreplaceable heritage of minerals from the great copper-mining days of Michigan's Keweenaw Peninsula, from Upper Peninsula iron-mining quarries, and Lower Peninsula dolostone and limestone quarries. Also displayed are minerals from other parts of North America, as well as Europe, China, Russia, and other worldwide mineral localities. The museum is the official "Mineralogical Museum of Michigan," and a charter Heritage Site for the Keweenaw National Historical Park. The museum's mission is to preserve minerals to educate and inspire future generations, and its vision is to be a dynamic museum of national prominence.

Admission: Free; donations appreciated.
Other services available: Mineral identification by prior arrangement. Gift shop.
Directions: The museum is located on the fifth floor of the Electrical Energy Resources Center (EERC) on the campus of the Michigan Technological University.

IRON MOUNTAIN

Mine Tour

Iron Mountain Iron Mine
P.O. Box 177
Iron Mountain, MI 49801
Phone: (906) 563-8077
Off-season: (906) 774-7914
E-mail: ironmine@uplogon.com
www.tm-arts.com/ironmine/ironmine.htm

Open: Memorial Day–October 15, 9:00 A.M.–5:00 P.M. Special arrangements can be made for groups.

Info: This is the largest public tour iron mine. Ride an underground mine train through 2,600 feet of underground drifts and tunnels to a depth of 400 feet below the earth's surface. Watch expert miners operate modern mining equipment. Get a free iron ore sample.

Admission: Adults $8.50, children 6–12 $6.50, children under 6 free.

Other services: Large and well-stocked rock and mineral gift shop, historical equipment display.

Directions: Located on U.S. 2 in Vulcan, 9 miles east of Iron Mountain.

LAKE LINDEN

Museum

Houghton County Historical Museum
P.O. Box 127
53102 Highway M-26
Lake Linden, MI 49945
Phone: (906) 296-4121
www.houghtonhistory.org

Open: June–September, 7 days/week, 10:00 A.M.–4:30 P.M. Special arrangements can be made for groups.

Info: The museum is located in the former main mill office of the Calumet & Hecla Mining Company, built in 1917. Displays include mining equipment and copper refining equipment.

Admission: Adults $8.00, children 12–18 and seniors $6.00, children 6–12 $4.00. Admission includes roundtrip train ride and access to campus trails and museum.

Other services available: The Historical Museum Complex includes eight historic buildings, on 15 acres of land, which depict life in the early days in the upper Michigan peninsula's copper country.

Directions: Located on Highway M-26 north from the Portage Lake Lift Bridge or south from Laurium.

MOHAWK

Mine Tour

Delaware Copper Mine
HCI, Box 102
Mohawk, MI 49950
Phone: (906) 289-4688
www.uptravel.com/attractions/copmine.htm

Open: June–October. September, October 10:00 A.M.–5:00 P.M., last tour at 4:15 P.M. June, July, August 10:00 A.M.–6:00 P.M., last tour at 5:15 P.M. Special arrangements can be made for groups.

Info: Tour an authentic copper mine that dates back to 1847. Two tours are available. (1) The self-guided tour, where you can take your time and examine the shafts and tunnels, runs from mid-May through June and from September through mid-October. (2) The guided tour goes down Shaft #1 to the first level at a depth of 110 feet, lasts about 45 minutes, and is followed by an above-ground walk through the mine site. The guided tour is offered in July and August.

Jackets and walking shoes are recommended, as it is 45°F in the mine. Searching for souvenir copper is allowed (no metal detectors).

Admission: Call for prices.

Other services available: Rock and mineral displays, refreshments, copper souvenirs, mini-zoo, mining displays, copper art, walking trails, antique engines, gift shop.

Directions: The mine is located in the historic ghost town of Delaware, which is 12 miles south of Copper Harbor and 38 miles north of Houghton on U.S. 41.

MOUNT PLEASANT

Museum 🏛

The Museum of Cultural and Natural History
Central Michigan University
103 Rowe Hall
Mount Pleasant, MI 48859
Phone: (989) 774-3829
E-mail: cmuseum@cmich.edu
www.museum.cmich.edu

Open: Monday–Friday 8:00 A.M.–5:00 P.M., closed noon–1:00 P.M.

Info: The museum has a small collection of rocks and minerals and includes a display of rocks and minerals of Michigan, as well as what is believed to be the largest Petoskey Stone ever found (420 pounds).

Admission: Free.

Directions: The museum is located in Rowe Hall, on Bellows Street just west of Business Route U.S. 27 (Mission Street). Park free in Lot 14 with a permit from the campus Department of Public Safety.

NEGAUNEE

Museum

Michigan Iron Industry Museum
73 Forge Road
Negaunee, MI 49866-9532

Phone: (906) 475-7857
www.michigan.gov/ironindustrymuseum

Open: May 1–October 15, 9:30 A.M.–4:30 P.M. 7 days/week. Call for additional dates in November and December.

Info: Dedicated to the story of Michigan's iron industry, which began in 1848 and continues today, the museum interprets Michigan's three iron ranges and the people who worked them. The museum overlooks the Carp River and the site of the first iron forge in the Lake Superior region. The museum features many exhibits, outdoor interpretive paths, and an 18-minute slide program, "Life on the Michigan Iron Ranges," which is shown in the auditorium. The Michigan Iron Industry Museum is part of the Michigan Historical Museum System.

Admission: Free.

Directions: The museum is located just off U.S. 41, 8 miles west of Marquette.

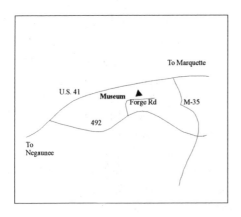

SHELBY

Factory Tour   🏛

Shelby Man-Made Gemstones
1330 Industrial Drive
Shelby, MI 49455
Phone: (231) 861-2165
Fax: (231) 861-6458
www.shelbygemfactory.com

Open: All year, 9:00 A.M.–5:30 P.M. Monday–Friday; noon– 4:00 P.M. Saturday.

Info: Visit a gemstone factory where artificial diamonds are created at an intense heat of 5040°F. Rubies, emeralds, and sapphires in various colors are also made here. Exhibits and shows in a 50-seat theatre present the story of artificial gemstones.

Admission: Free.

Other services available: Gift shop with a complete line of jewelry.

Directions: Shelby Man-Made Gemstones is located on Industrial Drive in Shelby. Take U.S. 31 north from Muskegon to the Shelby Road exit, then turn east on Shelby Road, then north onto 72nd Avenue. Turn east onto Woodrow Road, then north onto Industrial Park Drive.

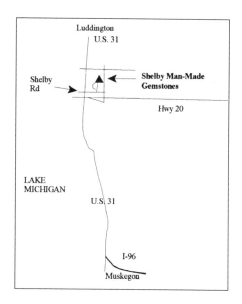

SECTION 3: Special Events and Tourist Information

ANNUAL EVENT

Copper County Mineral Retreat

The Copper County Mineral Retreat is a fun-filled, multi-faceted week for mineral collectors, mining history buffs, and rockhounds. The event takes place in the historic Lake Superior Copper District of Michigan's Keweenaw Peninsula, long recognized as the premier locality for crystallized native copper. Major retreat activities include mine tours of the Caledonia Mine, a geological tour, mineral swap, collecting field trips, slide presentations, and a benefit auction.

The retreat is sponsored by Red Metals Minerals, Quincy Mine Hoist Association, and the Copper Country Rock and Mineral Club. The event is hosted by Michigan Technological University.

TOURIST INFORMATION

State Tourist Agency

Travel Michigan
P.O. Box 30226
Lansing, MI 48909
Phone: (888) 784-7328;
(866) 644-2489
www.michigan.org

NEW HAMPSHIRE

State Gemstone: Smoky Quartz
State Mineral: Beryl
State Stone/Rock: Granite

GRAFTON / *Native ▪ Moderate to Difficult*

Collect up to 150 Different Minerals 𝑇

The following gems or minerals may be found:

▪ Mica, topaz, aquamarine, feldspar, beryl, chrysoberyl, amethyst and other quartz minerals, garnet, uranium minerals, tourmaline, columbite, molybdenite, pyrite, purpurite, zircon, and many others (See complete list below)

Ruggles Mine
Geraldine Searles
Off Rt. 4 at the Village Green
Grafton, NH 03240
Phone: (603) 523-4275
www.rugglesmine.com

Some of the Minerals Found at Ruggles Mine

Albite
Amethyst
Apatite
Autenite
Amphibolite
Aplite
Aquamarine
Bertranite
Beryl (golden, blue, aqua)
Beta-uranophane
Biotite
Bornite
Calcite
Chrysoberyl
Clarkite
Clevelandite
Columbite
Compotite
Cryolite
Cymatolite

Dendrite
Feldspar
Fluorapatite
Garnet
Gratonite
Gummite
Kasolite
Lepidolite (lemon yellow)
Lepidomelane
Lithiophylite
Marcasite
Manganapatite
Montmorillonite
Molybdenite
Muscovite
Parsonite
Phosphyanylite
Psilomelane
Purpurite
Pyrite

Pyrrhotite
Quartz (rose, smoky, white)
Reddingite
Safflorite
Sillmanite
Soddylite (pseudo-uranite, dense yellow)
Staurolite
Tobernite
Topaz crystals
Tourmaline (black)
Triphyllite
Uranite (species with gummite, world famous)
Uranium
Uranophane
Vandendriesscheite
Vivianite
Voelkerite
Zircon crystals

Secret of Ruggles Mine

It all began in 1803, back in the days of the whale oil lamp, when Sam Ruggles not only discovered mica on his land but knew what to do about it. Mica was in keen demand, for use in lamp chimneys and stove windows.

A shrewd hard-working farmer, he set his large family to working it out, and hauled it to Portsmouth by ox team along with his farm products. There it was consigned and shipped to relatives in England to be sold. (Ruggles was too shrewd to sell to American buyers lest they learn the secret of his mine.) Soon, however, the demand for his fine product became so great that special trips to the port were necessary. These were made in the dead of night by horse and buggy, or sleigh, according to season. This continued for several years.

The mine is famous for its huge books of mica, measuring 3–4 feet across and weighing over 100 pounds. General Electric once worked this mine and others in the area for mica. The Bon Ami Company operated the mine from 1932 to 1959 for feldspar, mica, and beryl. Feldspar production during this period ran about 10,000 tons per year. During this time, one mass of beryl was found that filled three freight cars and paid for an entire year's operation.

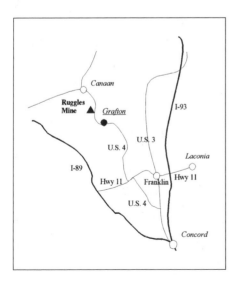

Open: Weekends, mid-May–mid-June; daily mid-June–mid-October; 9:00 A.M.–5:00 P.M., July and August 9:00 A.M.– 6:00 P.M. Last ticket sold 1 hour before closing.
Info: Commercial production of mica began in 1803 at the Ruggles Mine. It also is known for the production of beryl and feldspar. Located on the top of Isinglass Mountain, the mine now consists of open pits, giant rooms, and up to 1/3 mile of tunnels with arched ceilings. Its uranium minerals, such as gummite and autunite are prized by collectors and museums all over the world. Bring a camera—a vast

panorama of valleys, forest, and surrounding mountains can be seen from the top of the Isinglass Mountain. Unsurpassed fall foliage! A 2007 blasting revealed newly exposed minerals.

Admission: Adults $20.00/day, children 4–11 $10.00.

Other services available: Snack bar, gift and mineral shop, restrooms.

Note: Knowledge of mineral identification is a plus at this mine.

Directions: See website or call for directions.

LACONIA / *Native* ▪ *Moderate*

Collect Your Own Minerals *T*

The following gems or minerals may be found:

▪ **Amethyst, smoky quartz, quartz, mica**

Deer Hill Mineral Site
White Mountain National Forest
719 Main Street
Laconia, NH 03246
Phone: (603) 528-8721
Fax: (603) 528-8783
www.fs.fed.us/r9/forests/white_mountain
(Click on "Recreational Activities" on right side of page, then click on "Mineral Collecting.")

Open: All year, weather permitting.

Info: This is a rockhounding area in the White Mountain National Forest. Any one 18 years and older must have a permit for collecting. Permits can be obtained from either the Saco Ranger District [call (603) 447-5448 ext. 0];

the Androscoggin Ranger District [call (603) 466-2713]; or the Evans Notch Visitor Center [call (207) 824-2134].

Rates: Three permits are available: 1-day permit, $3.00; 10-day permit, $10.00; and 20-day permit, $20.00.

Directions: Call for directions to the site.

LACONIA / *Native* ▪ *Moderate*

Collect Your Own Minerals *T*

The following gems or minerals may be found:

▪ **Smoky quartz**

Moat Mountain Smoky Quartz Collecting Area
White Mountain National Forest
719 Main Street
Laconia, NH 03246
Phone: (603) 528-8721
Fax: (603) 528-8783
www.fs.fed.us/r9/forests/white_mountain
(Click on "Recreational Activities" on right side of page, then click on "Mineral Collecting.")

Open: All year, weather permitting.

Info: This is a well-known collecting site for smoky quartz. There is an information sheet available at the Saco Ranger District in Conway. Collecting at this location follows the forest standards and guidelines as outlined online.

Rates: Free.

Directions: A mineral brochure and general map are available online. Call for specific directions.

SECTION 2: Museums and Mine Tours

CONTOOCOOK

Museum

The Little Nature Museum
Gould Hill Orchards
656 Gould Hill Road
Contoocook, NH 03229
Phone: (603) 746-6123
E-mail: info@littlenaturemuseum.org
www.littlenaturemuseum.org

Open: June 28–October 26 on weekends and holidays; call for hours. Other times by appointment.
Info: The museum's collection includes rocks, ores, minerals, and fluorescent minerals.
Admission: Free; donations welcome.
Directions: From I-89, go through Hopkinton Village, and take Route 103 toward Contoocook. After 1¹⁄₂ miles, turn right on Gould Hill Road, and follow the signs.

DOVER

Museum

The Woodman Institute
182 Central Avenue
Dover, NH 03820
Phone: (603) 742-1038
www.woodmaninstitutemuseum.com

Open: Wednesday–Sunday (except holidays) 12:30–4:30 P.M.; closed December 1–March 31.
Info: The museum has 1,300 specimens of minerals and rocks on display, including a collection of local rocks in new display cases.
Admission: Adults $5.00, seniors 65+ $4.00, children 14–16 $2.00; under 14 free.
Directions: Take I-95 to Spaulding Turnpike, then take exit 7 to Central Avenue.

SECTION 3: Special Events and Tourist Information

TOURIST INFORMATION

State Tourist Agency

New Hampshire Division of Travel & Tourism Development
P.O. Box 1856
1172 Pembroke Road
Concord, NH 03302-1856

Phone: (603) 271-2665;
(800) FUN-INNH or (800) 386-4664
Fax: (603) 271-6870
www.visitnh.gov

NEW JERSEY

State Stone/Rock: Stockton Sandstone

CAPE MAY / *Native*

Hunt for Cape May "Diamonds" on the Beach *T*

The following gems or minerals may be found:

- Cape May "diamonds"

Cape May Welcome Center
Transportation Center
705 Lafayette Street
Cape May, NJ 08204
Phone: (609) 884-9562

Open: All year, dawn–dusk.

Info: Cape May "diamonds" are pure quartz crystals. Their source is the upper reaches of the Delaware River. Some 200 miles upstream from Cape May, pockets and veins of quartz have been eroded. During the thousands of years it takes for these pieces of quartz to make their way down the Delaware to the bay, they are worn smooth. The stones eventually find their way to the mouth of the bay, where strong currents move them along the shores. Eventually some of them wash ashore. The larger stones come ashore mostly in the winter months, particularly during storms, when the currents and waves are stronger. They can be found in abundance on Sunset Beach in historic Cape May Point; currents encounter the concrete ship *Atlantus* here, and the resulting eddies wash the "diamonds" ashore. When polished or cut and faceted, they are said to have the appearance of diamonds. Many people mount them into jewelry items.

Admission: Free.

Other attractions: Dolphin watching, concrete ship *Atlantus*, evening flag ceremony, spectacular sunsets, walking distance to lighthouse and state park.

Cape May "Diamonds" *

The gems are found in limited areas on the beaches along Delaware Bay. They are said to have first been found by the Kechmeche Indians. The Indians attached mystical powers to the stones and believed that these stones possessed supernatural powers, influencing the well-being, success, and good fortunes of the possessor. They often sealed bonds of friendship and goodwill with the gift of these stones.

For other areas where quartz "diamonds" can be found, see entries under Lakeport, CA, and Herkimer, Middleville, and St. Johnsville, NY.

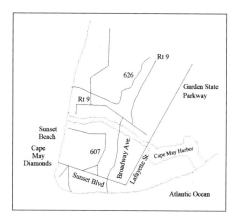

Directions: Sunset Beach in Cape May. Information and directions may be obtained by calling the Sunset Beach Gift Shops (609) 884-7079.

FRANKLIN / *Native · Easy*

Tailings Digging for Fluorescent Minerals *T*

The following gems or minerals may be found:

- Fluorescent minerals, franklinite

Franklin Mineral Museum and
Buckwheat Dump
32 Evans Street
Franklin, NJ 07416
Phone: (973) 827-3481
www.franklinmineralmuseum.com

Open: April–November, 10:00 A.M.–4:00 P.M. Monday–Friday; Saturday 10:00 A.M.–5:00 P.M.; 11:00 A.M.– 5:00 P.M. Sunday, closed Easter and Thanksgiving. Open to all visitors on March weekends and weekdays for groups by appointment. Collecting is available daily during operating hours. Special night digs are held the first Saturday of June and November.

Info: The "Buckwheat Dump" is located in "the fluorescent mineral capital of the world!" Collect rocks and minerals characteristic of the area. Find specimens and fluorescent minerals unique to the area on the mine waste pile which dates back to the 1870s. Facilities are available for testing specimens under ultraviolet light. Abundant specimens are available without the use of tools. A specimen exhibit in the testing facility and museum shows what to look for. Ultraviolet mineral lamps and other related items are for sale at the museum gift shop. See the listing in Section 2 for details on the Franklin Mineral Museum.

Admission: Fee charged.

Directions: 32 Evans Street off Route 23. Follow blue signs from Route 23 to Evans Street (between Main Street and Buckwheat Road).

OGDENSBURG / *Native • Moderate*

Collect Your Own Fluorescent Minerals

The following gems or minerals may be found:

- Fluorescent minerals

Sterling Hill Mine and Museum
30 Plant Street
Ogdensburg, NJ 07439
Phone: (973) 209-7212
Fax: (973) 209-8505
www.sterlinghill.org

Open: Mine dump collection area is open any day the museum is open. See the museum listing on p. 100. Collection is from 10:00 A.M. to 3:30 P.M. The pits are only open the last Sunday of the month.

Rates: $5.00 admission; $1.50 per pound collected. Not recommended for children under 8 years old.

Other services: See Ogdensburg entry in "Museums and Mine Tours" section.

SECTION 2: Museums and Mine Tours

FRANKLIN

Museum 🏛

Franklin Mineral Museum
32 Evans Street
Franklin, NJ 07416
Phone: (973) 827-3481
www.franklinmineralmuseum.com

Open: April–November, 10:00 A.M.– 4:00 P.M. Monday–Friday, 10:00 A.M.–5:00 P.M. Saturday, 11:00 A.M.– 5:00 P.M. Sunday. Closed Easter, Thanksgiving. Open to all visitors weekends in March, and weekdays for groups by appointment. Reservations are not required for visitors other than groups. Guided tours are offered hourly. Times adjusted during April through June and then again in September through November due to morning groups. Visitors are welcome to go through the museum exhibits on their own.

Info: The museum features minerals, rocks, geology, and replicas of mine workings. The specimens come from local and worldwide sources. The museum features a 33° fluorescent room, where various ores and minerals from the Franklin area are displayed under long-wave and short-wave ultraviolet light. Other displays feature specimens unique to the area and include gemstones and colorful crystals. The museum displays over 5,000 local specimens, some exclusive to the area, and 6,000 worldwide minerals. The Jensen wing contains the Welsh natural history collection. The mine replica is two levels containing mining artifacts. Items are featured throughout the museum regarding the mining history and mineralogy of the local area. The displays are impressive as well as educational.

The Franklin area was the site of iron and zinc mining from 1854 to 1954. Fluorescent minerals from the Franklin area are said to be the world's most brilliant, and specimens from this area are in museum collections all over the world. Franklin has been named "the fluorescent mineral capital of the world" by the state's legislature. The Franklin area has produced a tenth of all known species of minerals. (Species are still being identified today.) All displayed specimens are identified.

Admission: Fee charged.

Directions: 32 Evans Street off Route 23. Follow blue signs from Route 23 to Evans Street (between Main Street and Buckwheat Road).

MONROE TOWNSHIP

Museum

Displayworld's Stone Museum
Displayworld, Inc.
608 Spotswood-Englishtown Road
(Route 613)
Monroe Township, NJ 08831
Phone: (732) 521-2232
Fax: (732) 521-3388
E-mail:displayworld@erols.com
www.displayworld.com
(click on Stone Museum)

Open: April 1–December 23, 7 days/week. Monday–Saturday 8:00 A.M.–5:00 P.M.,

Sunday 10:00 A.M.–5:00 P.M. Closed Memorial Day, July 4, Labor Day.

Info: Museum of minerals (and fossils) with a host of indoor and outdoor displays that are "hands-on" so that visitors can actually touch specimens from 80 countries. Recent additions include an exhibit of fluorescent minerals from central New Jersey. Wander through the grounds and enjoy the lake and six stone waterfalls.

The museum is also a showcase of practical masonry. This 5-acre outdoor showroom has hundreds of full-size samples of every type of stone and stone product. Material on display is available for purchase.

The rock and gift shop contains a wide variety of polished gemstones, jewelry, fossils, collectibles, and carved products.

Admission: Free.

Directions: Garden State Parkway from the north: Take second exit south of Raritan toll plaza (exit 123—Route 9S); follow Route 9 south until you pass under Route 18 overpass, then take first right onto Texas Road (Route 520 West). Follow Route 520 to end, then turn left

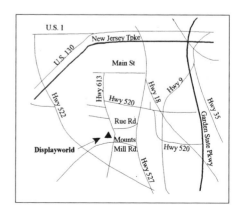

onto Route 613S; follow 2 miles to Displayworld on right.

From Turnpike exit 8A: Take Route 32 east to Jamesburg (Forsgate Drive), go about 2 miles to end, then right on Route 522E for 2 miles. Pass water tower on left, then drive 2 miles and turn left onto Route 613N. Follow Route 613N 2 miles to Displayworld.

From Turnpike exit 9: Take Route 18S, go about 9 miles to Route 9S. Take first right off Route 9 onto Texas Road (Route 520W), to end. Follow Route 520 to end, then turn left onto Route 613S; follow 2 miles to Displayworld on right.

MORRISTOWN

Museum

The Morris Museum
6 Normandy Heights Road
Morristown, NJ 07960
Phone: (973) 971-3700
www.morrismuseum.org

Open: All year, 10:00 A.M.–5:00 P.M. Tuesday–Saturday (open until 8:00 P.M. Thursday), 1:00–5:00 P.M. Sunday.

Info: The Rock and Mineral Gallery features specimens from five continents, and includes a calcite specimen weighing 258 pounds, and a giant amethyst. Exhibits explore the five geographic areas of the U.S., with emphasis on New Jersey. Another traces the path of a gem from raw material to precious stone. There is also a fluorescent mineral display.

Admission: Adults $8.00, children (3+) and seniors $6.00. Children under 3 free.

Admission is free to general public every Thursday between the hours of 5:00 P.M. and 8:00 P.M.

Directions: At 6 Normandy Heights Road, at the intersection with Columbia Turnpike in Morristown, NJ.

NEW BRUNSWICK

Museum

Rutgers Geology Museum
Geology Building
College Avenue Campus
New Brunswick, NJ 08903
Phone: (732) 932-7243
http://geology.rutgers.edu/museum/shtml

Open: While school is in session, Monday 1:00–4:00 P.M., Tuesday–Friday 9:00 A.M.–noon. Please call for weekend and summer hours.

Info: Museum features extensive mineral exhibits of specimens from the zinc deposits at Franklin, and zeolite deposits from Paterson. The gallery of meteorites includes a meteorite said to be from Mars.

Admission: Free.

Other services available: Small rock shop.

Directions: From the NJ Turnpike, take exit 9 and follow signs for Route 18 North—New Brunswick. Follow Route 18 for about 3 miles. Take the Route 27 South—Princeton exit onto Albany Street. At the third traffic light, turn right onto George Street. Proceed one block on George, pass through the railroad underpass, and proceed through the large iron gates on the corner of George and Som-

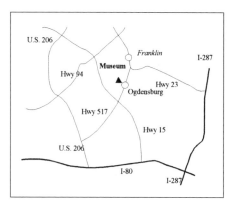

erset Streets. Parking is available in Lot 1.

If traveling from the south, take the Parkway north to exit 105 and follow the signs to Route 18—North, and follow as above.

If traveling from Route 287, take exit 9, Highland Park River Road. At the fifth light, in about 3 miles, at Metlars Lane, turn right and cross the Raritan River to New Brunswick on Route 18. Take the first exit, George Street. Proceed on George Street to the point where you pass under the railroad underpass, and follow as above.

OGDENSBURG

Museum/Mine Tour

Sterling Hill Mine and Museum
30 Plant Street
Ogdensburg, NJ 07439
Phone: (973) 209-7212
www.sterlinghill.org

Open: 7 days/week, April 1–November 30, December–March, weather permitting. Gift shop open 10:00 A.M.– 3:00 P.M. Tours daily at 1:00 P.M., other times by chance or appointment. Recommended for ages 6 and up. Group reservations required.

Info: Tour ¼ mile of mine tunnels in the last underground mine to operate in New Jersey. See a spectacular fluorescent mineral display in a natural environment. The museum's exhibit hall contains rare minerals, mining artifacts, and more. The Sterling Hill Mine is a National Historic Site; many original buildings remain, and mining equipment is on display. The mine tunnels are cool, a light jacket is recommended and proper footwear is required for the 1½–2-hour walking tour.

Admission: Adults $10.00, seniors $9.00, children 12 and under $7.50.

Other services available: Picnic area, snack bar, modern restrooms.

Directions: From Route 23 in Franklin, take Route 517 south to Ogdensburg. Turn right on Passaic Avenue and drive to the mine. From Route 15 in Sparta, take Route 517 north to Ogdensburg, then turn left onto Passaic Avenue, and drive to the mine.

Note: See information under Section one for fee dig at this site.

PATERSON

Museum

The Paterson Museum
Thomas Rogers Building
2 Market Street
Paterson, NJ 07501
Phone: (973) 321-1260
Fax: (973) 881-3435
E-mail: patersonmuseum@hotmail.com

Open: 10:00 A.M.– 4:00 P.M. Tuesday–Friday, 12:30 – 4:30 P.M. Saturday–Sunday, closed Mondays and holidays.

Info: There are two major mineralized basalt flows in the world: one in the Deccan plateau of India, and one in Paterson. The minerals found in both locations have much in common, but there are also significant differences. Many of the best and rarest Paterson specimens ever found are exhibited in the museum, along with many fine examples from the Poona region of India.

The museum's mineral collection is one of the finest exhibited collections in the state of New Jersey, with mineral specimens from the state and from around the world.

Admission: Suggested donation: Adults $2.00, children free.

Directions: The museum is located in the Thomas Rogers Locomotive Erecting Building, the focal point of the Great Falls Historic District, in close proximity to the Great Falls of the Passaic River. Paterson is on I-80 in northern New Jersey. Call for directions.

RUTHERFORD

Museum

Meadowland Museum
91 Crane Avenue
P.O. Box 3
Rutherford, NJ 07070
Phone: (201) 935-1175
Fax: (201) 935-9791
www.meadowlandsmuseum.org

Open: January–June, September–December, Monday and Wednesday 1:00–4:00 P.M., Sunday 2:00 –4:00 P.M. July–August, Monday–Thursday, 1:00 P.M.–4:00 P.M.; Sunday 2:00 P.M.–4:00 P.M. Call ahead to verify hours.

Info: Museum features a collection of fluorescent minerals, about half of which are from the Franklin Mine in New Jersey. The museum also has a display showing the many types of quartz. Another display shows the three types of rock (igneous, sedimentary, and metamorphic), while still another display presents minerals from the Paterson area. The museum also displays about 20 rocks/minerals from Snake Hill (Laurel Hill) in Secaucus, New Jersey.

Admission: Adults $2.00, children $1.00.

Directions: South on Route 17: turn right at Service Road/Local Streets sign, then turn right at Crane Avenue.

North on Route 17: Make jug-handle turn at Highland Cross, then follow directions above.

East on Route 3: Take Ridge Road exit, then turn left on Orient Way at second traffic light. Drive 2 blocks into Rutherford, and turn right on Crane Avenue.

West on Route 3: Take Ridge Road exit, then turn left at the stop sign. Turn left at the traffic light onto Rutherford Avenue, then turn left at the next light onto Orient Way. Go 3 blocks to Crane Avenue, and turn right.

TRENTON

Museum

New Jersey State Museum
Natural History Office, P.O. Box 530
205 West State Street
Trenton, NJ 08625-0530
Phone: (609) 292-6464
www.newjerseystatemuseum.org

Open: Tuesday–Saturday 9:00 A.M.–4:45 P.M., Sunday 12:00–5:00 P.M. Closed on state holidays.

Info: *Note:* Currently closed for renovations. Call to check for reopen date. The museum's geological collection contains minerals, rocks, sediments, and geological structures. The best mineral specimens are trap rock minerals and fluorescent Franklin/Sterling Hill samples. There is an extensive historic collection of magnetite ore samples from the old iron mines of New Jersey, many of which are closed or no longer exist.

Admission: Free. Parking is free.

Directions: The museum is located in two buildings on West State Street, which is reached by way of the Calhoun Street exit off Route 29.

SECTION 3: Special Events and Tourist Information

TOURIST INFORMATION

State Tourist Agency

New Jersey Division of Travel and Tourism

P.O. Box 460
20 West State Street
Trenton, NJ 08625-0826
Phone: (800) VISITNJ
www.visitnj.org

NEW YORK

State Gemstone: Garnet (1969)

HERKIMER / *Native ▪ Easy to Difficult*

Dig for Herkimer "Diamonds"

The following gems or minerals may be found:

▪ Herkimer "diamonds"

Herkimer Diamond Mine and KOA Kampground
800 Mohawk Street
Herkimer, NY 13350

Physical address:
4626 State Route 28 North
Herkimer, NY 13350
Phone: (315) 717-0175;
(866) 716-GEMS
Fax: (315) 717-0066
KOA reservations:
Phone: (315) 891-7355; (800) 562-0897
E-mail: diamonds@nchet.com

www.herkimerdiamond.com

Open: April 15–October 31, weather permitting, 9:00 A.M.–5:00 P.M., 7 days/week.
Info: Herkimer "diamonds" are quartz crystals found in specific locations in New York.

Bring your own tools or they will lend you a hammer. Suggested tools include various-sized chisels, a 3-pound hammer, a pry bar, eye protection, and gloves. For the very aggressive digger, a sledgehammer may be useful. Follow safety precautions. The "diamonds" may also be found by simply searching the ground or using a screenbox to sift the soil.
Admission: Ages 13 and up, $10.00/person; ages 5–12 $8.00/person; 4 and under free.
Other services available: Picnic area, playground, mineral museum containing thousands of specimens, gift and mineral shop.

KOA Kampground has cabins, cottages, tent sites, and RV sites with water, sewer, and electrical hookups. Modern restrooms and showers, ice and firewood, fishing, tubing, swimming, miniature golf, playgrounds, and restaurant are available. Call for rates.
Directions: From the NYS Thruway, use exit 30 and take State Highway 28 north. Herkimer Diamond Mines is 7 miles north of Herkimer.

MIDDLEVILLE / *Native • Easy to Difficult*

Prospect for Herkimer "Diamonds"

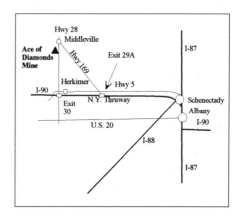

The following gems or minerals may be found:

- Herkimer "diamonds," calcite crystals, dolomite crystals

Ace of Diamonds Mine and
Campground
Ted and Anita Smith
P.O. Box 505
Middleville, NY 13406
Phone: (315) 891-3855; (315) 891-3896
www.herkimerdiamonds.com

Open: April 1–October 31, 9:00 A.M.–5:00 P.M., 7 days/week.

Info: Bring your own tools or rent tools at the mine. Suggested tools include a small shovel, a pick, a garden rake or a trowel, a 2½-pound hammer, and a bucket. You may want to bring gloves or kneeling pad, and a screenbox.

To stake a claim, place a blue tarp or tools in your area, not to exceed 10 feet. You may pay in advance to keep your claim from day to day.

The mine's conservation rule is as follows: One pocket only per person or group. After cleaning out the pocket, the digger or group must leave the mine for 2 weeks, or a $75.00 trophy fee may be paid by the successful prospector or

---

Herkimer "Diamonds"

Herkimer "diamonds" are very brilliant, clear, quartz crystals, which are double-terminated (points on both ends) and six-sided. They appear to be faceted by nature, and many are used in jewelry. Rare ones are found with liquid bubble inclusions. They range in size from microscopic to several inches. They are found in a rock formation known as dolomite. The crystals are found mostly in pockets in the rock; many others, however, are found in the surrounding soil.

Also see listings under Lakeport, CA, for moon tears, or Lake County "diamonds," and Cape May, NJ, for Cape May "diamonds."

---

group in order to continue mining for a second pocket. If a second pocket is obtained, then the person or group must leave the mine for 2 weeks. The following activities are not allowed at any time: using sledgehammers over 12 pounds, using hydraulic jacks in the mining areas, rolling boulders down the slopes, and breaking rocks in the camping areas.

Admission: Age 8 and above, $7.50/day; 7 and under, $4.00/day. Take home all the "diamonds" and specimens you find. Group rates are available (school children with adult supervision $6.00/person, college student and adult groups $7.00/person). To rent long-handled tools at the mine, $1.00 each; sledgehammer, $4.00 each. Deposit or driver's license is required for tool rental. New tools are offered for sale.

Other services available: Picnic area, snack shop, rock shop, restrooms, camping right where you dig. Within walking distance: luncheonette, grocery store, post office, trout fishing.

Note: All collecting is done at your own risk. The mine is not responsible for injury or loss of personal property.

Campground: $10.00/night for each vehicle and two people, additional people $1.00/night, $3.00/night for electrical hookup, free water hookup, bathrooms with coin-operated showers.

Directions: From the NY Thruway, use exit 30, and take State Highway 28 north. Ace of Diamonds Mines is 9 miles north of Herkimer.

Herkimer "diamonds" can be found simply by walking around the prospecting area or using a screenbox to sift dirt in the prospecting area. The most popular method is breaking them out of the rock. A few rules must be followed:

Herkimer "Diamonds"

- Wear eye protection.
- Never break rocks close to someone else. Look in all directions before hammering.
- Keep a close eye on children. Never allow them on top of any high wall or cliff.

> A 23-ton block of matrix rock from the Barton Garnet Mine has been cut and polished, and transported to Ground Zero at the World Trade Center in New York City. It will be the corner stone of the new World Trade Center and, until then, is on display.

NORTH RIVER / *Native • Moderate*

Collect Garnets in a Historic New York Garnet Mine *T*

The following gems or minerals may be found:

- Garnets

The Barton Mine
Bonnie and Peter Barton
P.O. Box 30
North River, NY 12856
Phone: (518) 251-2706
www.garnetminetours.com

Open: July–Labor Day, 9:30 A.M.–5:00 P.M. Monday–Saturday, 11:00 A.M.–5:00 P.M. Sunday. Labor Day–Columbus Day open on weekends only. Groups may arrange tours during the week.

Info: The Barton Mine is called the world's largest garnet mine and has the world's hardest garnet. The admission fee includes a guided tour of the mine, followed by a demonstration on how to find your own garnets.

Admission: Adults $10.00, children $6.50, seniors $8.50.

Other services available: Mineral shop, picnic tables.

Directions: From Interstate 87, take Exit 23 to Route 9. Follow Route 9 to Route 28, and take Route 28 for approximately 21 miles to North River. At the North River General Store, turn left onto Barton Mine Road. The mine is approximately 5 miles from North River.

ST. JOHNSVILLE / *Native • Easy to Difficult*

Dig for Herkimer "Diamonds" *T*

The following gems or minerals may be found:

- Herkimer "diamonds"

Crystal Grove Diamond Mine and Campground
161 County Highway 114
St. Johnsville, NY 13452
Phone: (518) 568-2914;
(800) KRY-DIAM or (800) 579-3426
E-mail: fun@crystalgrove.com
www.crystalgrove.com

Open: April 15–October 15, 8:00 A.M.–dusk, 7 days/week.

Info: Use a shovel, hammer and chisel, or small garden tool. If you would rather not break rocks, sifting the dirt through a screenbox will also reveal these gems. Bring your own tools, or some rental tools are available. Suggested tools include various-sized chisels, a 3-pound hammer, a pry bar, eye protection, and gloves. For the very aggressive digger, a sledgehammer may be useful.

Admission: Adults $10.00/day, children under 14 $8.00/day. Group rates available.

Other services available: Picnic area, playground, rock shop with mineral and rock specimens from all over the world. A wooded campground, located at the foothills of the beautiful Adirondacks, is adjacent to the mine. It has water and electrical sites, tent sites, dump station, modern restrooms and showers, ice and firewood, playground, horseshoe pit, volleyball, basketball, ping-pong. There are many nearby attractions. Rates: $25.00 to $32.00 per day (four people), extra charge for additional persons.

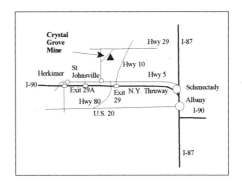

Camping cabins for 4–6 people are also available.

Directions: From the NY Thruway, use exit 29 or exit 29A and go to St. Johnsville. Turn at traffic light (Division Street) and travel north ½ mile to a fork in the road. Take the right fork for 4 miles to the campsite. From the north, get on Route 29 to County Road 114. Take 114 south to the mine.

SECTION 2: **Museums and Mine Tours**

ALBANY

Museum

New York State Museum
Room 3023
Cultural Education Center
Albany, NY 12230
Phone: (518) 474-5877
www.nysm.nysed.gov

Open: All year, daily, 9:30 A.M.–5:00 P.M. Closed major holidays.

Info: Exhibits include "Minerals from New York" and "Ancient Life of New York—a Billion Years of Earth History." The minerals in the "Minerals from New York" exhibit will be rotated periodically.

Admission: Free. Suggested donation of $2.00/person.

Directions: The museum is located in the Cultural Education Center of the Empire State Plaza in Albany, on Madison Avenue across the Plaza from the State Capitol Building. Parking is available at two lots adjacent to the museum; parking there is free after 3:00 P.M.

HICKSVILLE

Museum

The Hicksville Gregory Museum
Long Island Earth Science Center
1 Heitz Place
Hicksville, NY 11801-3101
Phone: (516) 822-7505
Fax: (516) 822-3227
E-mail: gregorymuseum@earthlink.net
www.gregorymuseum.org

Open: All year, 9:30 A.M.–4:30 P.M.
Tuesday–Friday, 1:00–5:00 P.M. Saturday
and Sunday, closed Monday. Groups by
appointment.

Info: The mineral collection has approximately 10,000 specimens. Only a small
number are on display at any one time.
The permanent display features a sampling that serves as an introduction to the
major mineral groups. It includes many
economically important minerals. Also on
display are New Jersey zeolites, Herkimer
"diamonds," and fluorescent minerals.

Admission: Adults $5.00, children and
seniors $3.00.

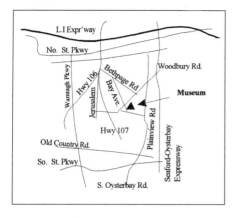

Special programs offered include
school programs, teacher training, science and craft workshops, and merit
badge programs for Girl Scouts and Boy
Scouts.

Directions: Located at the Heitz Place
Courthouse.

NEW YORK CITY

Museum

American Museum of Natural History
Central Park West at 79th Street
New York, NY 10024
Phone: (212) 769-5100
Fax: (212) 769-5427
www.amnh.org

Open: All year, 10:00 A.M.–5:45 P.M.
daily, closed Thanksgiving and Christmas. Groups by appointment.

Info: The natural history of our planet
and its species is revealed in more than
40 exhibit halls. The Morgan Memorial
Hall of Gems features the Star of India,
the world's largest and most famous
blue star sapphire. Among other permanent halls is the Arthur Ross Hall of
Meteorites, which features the 4½-bil-
lion-year-old Ahnighito, the largest
meteorite ever retrieved from the
earth's surface.

Admission: Adults $15.00, students and
seniors $11.00, children 2–12 $8.50.

Other services available: Museum
shops, restaurants, discovery room for
children, theatre, and planetarium.

PAWLING

Museum

Akin Free Library
The Gunnison Natural History Museum
Quaker Hill
397 Old Quaker Hill Road
P.O. Box 345
Pawling, NY 12564
Phone: (914) 855-5099

Open: May 15–October 15, 2:00–4:00
P.M. Thursday–Sunday. Groups by appointment.
Info: This natural history museum was presented to the community by Olive Mason Gunnison, whose collection covers all phases of natural history. The mineral sections are outstanding, and complete information on each specimen is provided.
Admission: Adults $1.00, children $0.50.
Other services available: Historical museum, Akin Free Library.
Directions: Pawling is located on State Highway 22, 13 miles north of I-84, near the NY–CT border. The library can be reached by taking Quaker Hill Road 3 miles east from Pawling.

SECTION 3: Special Events and Tourist Information

TOURIST INFORMATION

State Tourist Agency

New York Division of Tourism
30 South Pearl Street
Albany, NY 12245
Phone: (800) CALL NYS; (518) 479-4116 or (800) 225-5697
www.iloveny.com

Ohio Flint

Centuries ago, Native Americans from throughout the Midwest forged trails to a range of hills, about 10 miles long, located between the present cities of Newark and Zanesville, Ohio. They came to these hills to obtain flint, and the area came to be known as Flint Ridge. They used the flint to make implements to kill and skin game and to make weapons. The flint in this area occurs in shades of pink, gray, white, yellow, orange, black, and multicolored.

Quarrying for flint was hard work. The flint on the surface exposed to the elements cracked easily; below the surface, a layer of material between 1 and 10 feet deep was of high quality. Large hammerstones weighing up to 25 pounds were used to drive wedges into natural cracks in the flint layer to break large pieces off. Smaller stones were then used to break workable pieces of flint, which were finished as tools or weapons.

Extensive trading networks established by the Hopewell people spread items from Flint Ridge across the eastern half of the country in exchange for such things as copper from the upper Great Lakes and shells from the Gulf of Mexico.

White settlers in the area used the lower grade of weathered flint for making buhrstones for water-powered mills. Smaller pieces were used for hand grinding.

Today, Ohio flint, which is a form of chalcedony, is used by jewelry makers, who polish it and make it into items such as pendants and belt buckles.

For information on other Native American stone quarries, see listings in Newark, DE: jasper quarries (Vol. 4); Calumet and Copper Harbor, MI: copper (Vol. 4); Pipestone, MN: pipestone quarries (Vol.1); and Fritch, TX: flint quarries (Vol. 2).

OHIO

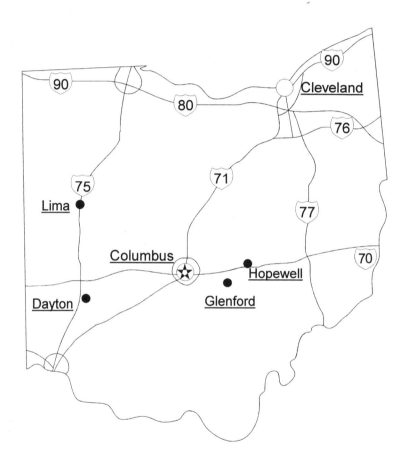

State Gemstone: Flint (1965)

HOPEWELL / *Native • Easy to Difficult*

Dig for Flint 〒

The following gems or minerals may be found:

▪ Ohio flint

Hidden Springs Ranch
Gene Wyrick
9305 Hidden Springs Road
Hopewell, OH 43746
Phone: (740) 787-2060
E-mail: gwgenie@alltel.net

Open: By appointment in advance; limited to groups. 8:00 A.M.–8:00 P.M., 7 days/week.

Info: Dig for Ohio flint in a prehistoric Indian flint quarry. Flint occurs in a hard rock environment, so bring appropriate equipment, including safety goggles and gloves. Bring your own 5-gallon bucket! The ranch can accommodate a maximum of 35 people in a group.

Admission: $6.00/person, $6.00 per 5-gallon bucket of flint removed, $60.00

nonrefundable deposit required.

Other services available: Hay rides; outdoor barbecues; stocked fishing lake; outhouses; square dancing; wood for campfires; horseback trail ride; cross-country skiing; campground (primitive campsites for use by tents or campers, $5.00/night) with reservation.

Directions: Send a stamped self-addressed envelope for specific directions to the ranch.

HOPEWELL / *Native • Easy to Difficult*

Dig for Flint 〒

The following gems or minerals may be found:

▪ Ohio flint

Nethers Flint
John Nethers
3680 Flint Ridge Road
Hopewell, OH 43746
Phone: (740) 787-2263

Open: All year, weather permitting, daylight hours.

Info: Dig or find your own flint in a wooded ancient quarry area across from the farmhouse. Remember, flint is very sharp. See the safety notes below.

Admission: $5.00/person for the first 10 pounds, $0.50/pound above 10 pounds. Bring your own tools and protective equipment.

How to Dig for Flint

Today, one can obtain flint in much the same way those Native Americans did centuries ago. The only difference is that today you can use implements made of steel instead of stone.

Because most of the flint is several feet underground, the overlying soil must be removed to expose the flint. There is flint on the surface in some areas, but it is weathered and cracks easily. The normal method used to expose the flint is to dig a pit. (From the numerous ancient pits observable at the various sites, it is obvious that this is what the Native Americans did.) This exposed flint can then be chipped away.

Quarrying for flint is still hard work unless you go the easy route that the authors used and pick through pieces lying in the pits from previous quarrying. The authors collected 65 pounds of flint in varying colors of pink, orange, red, yellow, white, black, and gray. Many pieces contained quartz crystals; even some individual quartz crystals were found. They plan to make cabochons from some of the nice pieces!

Caution: There is a reason why flint was used by Native Americans to make weapons—it can be very sharp. Appropriate caution should be taken, especially if children are involved in the collection. Safety glasses or goggles, gloves, and hard-sided/hard-soled boots should be worn. Care should be taken when working in the "pits" to ensure that the earthen walls do not collapse. *Note:* the authors' daughter, Annie, 9 years old at the time, collected flint, did a little quarrying, and even tried to make an arrowhead, without a scratch.

Note: The Nethers allow flint collecting on their farm, but the collecting is at your own risk. No liability is assumed by the owners.

Directions: I-70 to Brownsville-Gratiot exit. Turn left on SR 668 to Route 40. Turn right on Route 40 to Hopewell School. Just past the school, turn left on County Line Road and travel about 3 miles to Mt. Olive Road, on the left, and Flint Ridge Road (ahead to left). Turn onto Flint Ridge Road and travel 1.2 miles; stop at the white two-story house on the right to pay. The collecting area is on the left. If coming from Zanesville on I-70, take exit 152 to Route 40; turn right on Route 40 and travel approximately 9 miles to Hopewell School; turn right on County Line Road and follow the directions above.

CLEVELAND

Museum 🏛

The Cleveland Museum of Natural History
Wade Gallery of Gems and Minerals
1 Wade Oval Drive, University Circle
Cleveland, OH 44106-1767
Phone: (216) 231-4600; (800) 317-9155
Fax: (216) 231-5919
E-mail: info@cmnh.org
www.cmnh.org

Open: Monday–Saturday 10:00 A.M.–5:00 P.M., Wednesday 10:00 A.M.–10:00 P.M., Sunday noon–5:00 P.M. Closed major holidays.

Info: The Wade Gallery of Gems and Minerals opened May 9, 1998, showcasing more than 1,500 gems, jewels, and treasures. The collection is considered to be one of the top five institutionally owned collections in the United States.

The Wade collection includes more than 50 types of gemstones, including colored diamonds, opals, rubies, sapphires, emeralds, pearls, and jade, all of which are now on permanent display. The colored diamonds range from deep, clear green to pale orchid, pink, orange, brown, and blue. The collection also contains one of the largest groups of opals in the country, including black opal from Australia, fire opal from Mexico, and vibrant colored opals from Nevada's Virgin Valley. Jeptha Homer Wade, II, was a Cleveland businessman, philanthropist, and collector of gems and minerals. He was the grandson of the founder of Western Union and was among the first members of the board of directors of the museum. Wade acquired much of his collection with the purpose of donating it to the museum. His granddaughter and grandson have made further donations to his collection.

The jewelry on display ranges from pendants, necklaces, brooches, and bracelets to diamond, gold, and opal rings. Two striking necklaces on display are a rare emerald necklace anecdotally dated to the 1700s, and a topaz and diamond necklace created in 1905 by Tiffany jewelers. The new gallery also presents the spectacular Davidson collection of mineral eggs and cabochons.

Admission: Adults $9.00; children

7–18, seniors 60+, and students $7.00; ages 3–6 $6.00.

Other services available: Museum store.

Directions: Take Euclid or Chester Avenue east from I-90/I-71/I-77.

COLUMBUS

Museum

Orton Geological Museum
Ohio State University
155 South Oval
Columbus, OH 43210
Phone: (614) 292-6896
www.geology.ohio-state.edu/facilities.php

Open: Monday–Friday 9:00 A.M.–5:00 P.M. Weekend and evening hours by special request.

Info: The museum features geology of Ohio, showing rocks and minerals from the state. Also includes specimens from all over the world. Other exhibits include meteorites (including one that fell in Ohio), minerals, crystals, and fluorescent minerals.

Exhibits illustrate the fundamental concepts about minerals and their physical properties. From the clay tiles in the entrance hall to its wall and foundations, Orton Hall is built of 40 different Ohio building stones.

Admission: Free.

Other services: Free identification of rocks and minerals, museum store.

Directions: Located in Orton Hall on the campus of Ohio State University in Columbus.

DAYTON

Museum

Boonshoft Museum of Discovery
2600 DeWeese Parkway
Dayton, OH 45414
Phone: (937) 275-7431
Fax: (937) 275-3811
www.boonshoftmuseum.org

Open: Monday–Friday 9:00 A.M.–5:00 P.M., Saturday 11:00 A.M.–5:00 P.M, Sunday 12:00–5:00 P.M.

Info: Many crystals and minerals are on display in the Bieser Discovery Center, a hands-on area of the museum.

Admission: Adults $8.50, seniors $7.00, children 2–12 $7.00, under 2 free.

Other services available: Zoo, children's play area, space theatre.

Directions: From I-75, take exit 57B (Wagner Ford–Siebenthaler exit). Go west on Wagner Ford Road to North Dixie Drive to Siebenthaler Avenue to Ridge Avenue to DeWeese Parkway. Watch for signs.

GLENFORD

Museum 🏛

Flint Ridge State Memorial
7091 Brownsville Road SE
Glenford, OH 43739
Phone: (740) 787-2476; (800) 283-8707

Open: Park and museum open Memorial Day–Labor Day, Wednesday–Saturday 9:30 A.M.–5:00 P.M.; Sundays and holidays noon–5:00 P.M. School groups and bus

Admission: Adults $4.00, students 6–12 $3.00, children under 6 free.

Directions: Located at the intersection of County Road 312 (Flint Ridge Road) and County Road 668 (Brownsville Road), 3 miles north of Brownsville, Ohio, and 5 miles north of I-70.

LIMA

Museum

Allen County Museum
Allen County Historical Society
620 West Market Street
Lima, OH 45801
Phone: (419) 222-9426
Fax: (419) 222-0649
www.allencountymuseum.org

Open: June–August, Tuesday–Saturday 10:00–5:00 P.M., Sundays 1:00 P.M.–5:00 P.M., closed Mondays and national holidays.

Info: The museum features an extensive rock and mineral collection, with an entire room solely for the mineral display.

Admission: Free. Suggested donation: $5.00/adult.

Other services available: Library, children's museum, garden, railroad, archives, and Victorian "MacDonell House."

Directions: Northwest of the intersection of State Highways 309 and 65 in Lima.

tours by appointment all year.

Info: In 1933, the Ohio Historical Society established the Flint Ridge State Memorial. In 1968, a museum was constructed over one of the original quarry pits (see discussion on Ohio flint at the beginning of this chapter). Exhibits present the geology and history of the site, and the location of other flint deposits in Ohio. In the ancient mining pit, life-sized mannequins show how the material was quarried and then worked to make tools and weapons.

The museum displays a variety of objects made of flint. The shop features flint as a gemstone with locally crafted jewelry. Also sold are books and gifts related to prehistoric Ohio.

A nature preserve with walking trails is located at the memorial. An asphalt path with handrails is available for the handicapped. Also provided are Braille and standard text signs.

SECTION 3: Special Events and Tourist Information

TOURIST INFORMATION

State Tourist Agency

Ohio Division of Travel and Tourism
P.O. Box 1001
Columbus, OH 43216-1001
Phone: (800) BUCKEYE or
(800) 282-5393
www.ohiotourism.com

PENNSYLVANIA

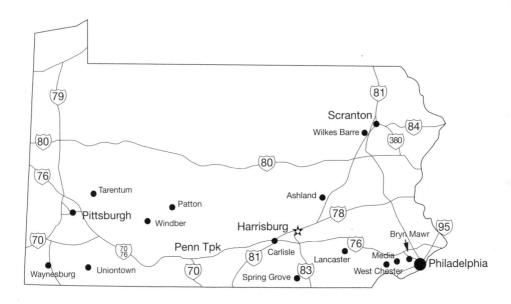

State Stone/Rock: Trilobite

SECTION 1: Fee Dig Sites and Guide Services

SPRING GROVE

Guide Services for Mineral Collecting *T*

The following gems or minerals may be found:

- Gold, various minerals

Jeri Jones
Jones Geological Services
2223 Stoverstown Road
Spring Grove, PA 17362
Phone: (717) 225-3744

E-mail: jlj276@aol.com or jjones@jonesgeo.com
www.jonesgeo.com

Open: By appointment.
Info: Mr. Jones offers a variety of field trips and collecting tours, which he can tailor to your needs. Also offered is a gold-panning program.
Rates: Call for rates.
Other services offered: A variety of publications on southeastern Pennsylvania geology are available on his website.

> A free gold-panning program is presented at Spring Valley County Park the last Saturday of July from 9:00 A.M.–2:00 P.M.

SECTION 2: Museums and Mine Tours

ASHLAND

Museum

Museum of Anthracite Mining
Pennsylvania Museum and Historical Commission/Borough of Ashland
17th and Pine Streets
Ashland, PA 17921
Phone: (570) 875-2411
www.phmc.state.pa.us/bhsm/toh/anthmining/anthracite.asp

Open: Monday–Friday, 8:00 A.M.–5:00 P.M.
Info: Exhibits and displays present the story of mining and processing anthracite coal.

Admission: Adults $4.00, children 6–17 $2.00, seniors over 60 $3.50.
Directions: From I-80, take I-81 to exit 36W (Frackville exit). Take PA Route 61 north to Ashland. From I-78, take PA Route 61 north to Ashland.

ASHLAND

Mine Tour

Pioneer Tunnel Coal Mine
Ashland Community Enterprise
19th and Oak Streets
Ashland, PA 17921
Phone: (570) 875-3850; (570) 875-3301
www.pioneertunnel.com

Open: Memorial Day–Labor Day 10:00 A.M.–6:00 P.M. Check website for off-season days/times.

Info: Visit an actual coal mine in the heart of Pennsylvania's anthracite region. Pioneer Tunnel is a horizontal drift mine, which runs 1,800 feet straight into the side of Nahanoy Mountain. Ride in open mine cars pulled by a battery-operated mine motor deep inside the mountain. The mine tour temperature averages 50°F throughout the tour, so bring your sweater or jacket (if necessary, one will be provided to you during the tour).

Admission: Adults $8.00, children under 12 $5.50. Group rates available.

Other services available: Ride an old-fashioned narrow-gauge steam locomotive–powered mine train. See a strip mine, "bootleg" coal hole, and Ashland, a typical early 1900s mining town. Playground and picnic area, gift shop and snack bar. Call for fees.

Directions: From I-80, take I-81 to exit 124B (Frackville exit). Take PA Route 61 north to Ashland. From I-78, take PA Route 61 north to Ashland.

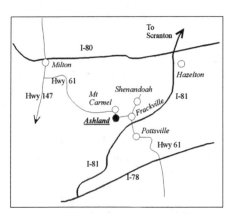

BRYN MAWR

Museum 🏛

Department of Geology
Park Science Building
Bryn Mawr College
Bryn Mawr, PA 19010
Phone: (610) 526-5115
Fax: (610) 526-5086

Open: September 1–May 15 (academic year), 9:00 A.M.–5:00 P.M. Other times of the year by appointment. Group or guided tours available by calling.

Info: View the 1,500 minerals on display in the halls. Approximately 23,500 additional specimens are in the storage rooms.

Admission: Free.

Directions: Bryn Mawr College is located just west of Philadelphia, on U.S. 30. Park in the Science Center lot on New Gulph Road between Roberts Road and Morris Avenue, off Montgomery Avenue near the Bryn Mawr train station. Obtain a parking permit from the public safety building.

CARLISLE

Museum

Rennie Geology Museum
Department of Geology
Dickinson College
Kaufman Building
P.O. Box 1773
Carlisle, PA 17013-2896
Phone: (717) 245-1448
Fax: (717) 245-1971
http://alpha.dickinson.edu/
departments/geol/rennie/rennie.html

Open: Monday–Friday, 8:00 A.M.–5:00 P.M.
Info: After being renovated, the museum will reopen in the summer of 2008. Call to find out the exact date of reopening. The museum, located on the first floor of the Kaufman Building, contains three cases displaying minerals and one case displaying gems. There is also a fluorescent mineral display and a digital, live seismometer.
Admission: Free.
Directions: From Interstate 81, take exit 49 (High Street), bear right at the traffic light, and drive into downtown Carlisle. Go through the square at Hanover

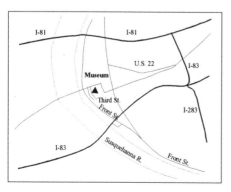

Street and continue for a few blocks until you get to Cherry Street. Turn right onto Cherry Street. The Kaufman Building is on the second block on the right. Parking is available on the street and the museum is on the first floor. The Kaufman Building is located at the corner of Cherry Street and West Lauther Street.

HARRISBURG

Museum

The State Museum of Pennsylvania
300 North Street
Harrisburg, PA 17120
Phone: (717) 787-4980
http://www.statemuseumpa.org

Open: 9:00 A.M.–5:00 P.M. Tuesday–Saturday, noon–5:00 P.M. Sunday.
Info: Exhibits and displays explain the basic concepts of geology. Visitors learn about practical applications of geology in displays that present information on materials extracted from rocks, and the everyday products that result.
Admission: Free.
Directions: At the intersection of Third Street and North Street, in Harrisburg, at the capitol complex.

LANCASTER

Museum

North Museum of Natural History and Science
400 College Avenue
Lancaster, PA 17603

Phone: (717) 291-3941
E-mail: info@northmuseum.org
www.northmuseum.org

Open: 9:00 A.M.–5:00 P.M. Tuesday–Saturday, 12:00–5:00 P.M. Sunday.

Info: The museum has an extensive geology collection with a large number of rocks and minerals on display. Other exhibits include Dinosaur Hall, discovery room, live animal room, birds, shells, insects, Native American, and more.

Admission: Adults $5.50, children 3–12 and seniors over 65 $4.50. Planeterium show $3.50.

Directions: In Lancaster, on the campus of Franklin and Marshall College, at the corner of College and Buchanan Avenues.

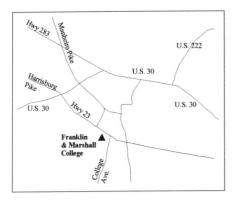

LANSFORD

Mine Tour/Museum

No. 9 Mine & Museum
9 Dock Street
P.O. Box 287
Lansford, PA 18232
Phone: (570) 645-7074
www.no9mine.com

Open: Museum is open all year, Wednesday to Sunday, noon–4:00 P.M. (Note: hours may change in the off-season.) Mine: May–October 31. May: Friday–Sunday, tours from 11:00 A.M.–3:15 P.M.; June–Labor Day: Thursday–Sunday, tours from 11:00 A.M.–3:15 P.M.; Labor Day–end of October: Saturday–Sunday, tours from 11:00 A.M.–3:15 P.M.

Info: This anthracite coal mine operated from 1855 to 1972, and was reopened as a tour mine in 2002. Ride a tram 1600 feet into the mine and see how the miners worked. The museum exhibits chronicle nearly 200 years of mining in the Panther Valley.

Admission: Mine tour and museum, $7.00; museum only, $3.00.

Other services available: Picnic grove, gift shop.

Directions: Located in Lansford, just off U.S. Route 209 at the Lansford/Coaldale border.

MEDIA

Museum

Delaware County Institute of Science
11 Veterans Square
Media, PA 19063
Phone: (610) 566-5126
http://www.delcohistory.org/dcis

Open: Monday, Thursday, and most Saturdays 9:00 A.M.–1:00 P.M., excluding holidays.

Arrangements for group tours can be

made by calling the institute.

Info: Display and research collection contains hundreds of minerals from around the world. Many minerals from famous localities in the area are included. The museum houses the original plate blocks used to print Dr. Samuel Gordon's 1922 *Mineralogy of Pennsylvania*. Specimens brought from the mineral prospects of the West by members of the Delaware County Institute of Science during the 1800s can be viewed and studied.

Admission: Free.

Directions: The institute is located in the center of Media near the county courthouse. Media is located west of Philadelphia, near U.S. 1.

PATTON

Mine Tour/Museum

Seldom Seen Mine
P.O. Box 83
Patton, PA 16668
Phone: (814) 247-6305
Off-season/days closed: (814) 674-8939
www.seldomseenmine.com

Open: July and August, Thursday–Sunday; June, Saturday and Sunday, noon–5:00 P.M. May, September, and October, scheduled tours for groups of 25 or more only. Check website or call for days and times.

Info: Tour an underground bituminous coal mine. Ride an electric mine train into the mine. During the tour, your guide will discuss the past, present, and future of coal mining. Aboveground, view a theatre presentation or tour the museum to learn more about mining.

Admission: Adults $7.00, children 3–12 $4.00.

Directions: Located on Route 36, 4 miles north of Patton.

PHILADELPHIA

Museum

Academy of Natural Science
1900 Benjamin Franklin Parkway
Philadelphia, PA 19103
Phone: (215) 299-1000
www.acnatsci.org

Open: All year, Monday–Friday, 10:00 A.M.–4:30 P.M. Saturdays, Sundays, holidays 10:00 A.M.–5:00 P.M.; closed Thanksgiving and Christmas.

Info: The academy has a permanent

exhibit of gems and minerals.

Rates: Adults $10.00, seniors and military $8.50, children 3–12 $8.00.

Other services: Gift shop.

Directions: See website or call for directions.

PHILADELPHIA

Museum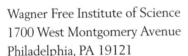

Wagner Free Institute of Science
1700 West Montgomery Avenue
Philadelphia, PA 19121
Phone: (215) 763-6529
Fax: (215) 763-1299
www.wagnerfreeinstitute.org

Open: Tuesday–Friday, 9:00 A.M.– 4:00 P.M. Arrangements for group tours can be made by calling ahead.

Info: The institute houses an extensive collection of more than 100,000 natural history specimens, including rocks and minerals.

Admission: Free.

Directions: Take the Broad Street exit off I-676. Follow Broad Street north to Norris Street, and turn left at Norris. Go three blocks to 17th Street, turn left, and go one block to Montgomery Avenue.

PITTSBURGH

Museum

Carnegie Museum of Natural History
4400 Forbes Avenue
Pittsburgh, PA 15213

Phone: (412) 622-3131
E-mail: cmnhweb@carnegiemnh.org
www.carnegiemnh.org

Open: Year round; closed major holidays. 10:00 A.M.–5:00 P.M. Tuesday–Saturday (10:00 A.M.–5:00 P.M. Monday between July 4 and Labor Day, otherwise, closed Mondays), 10:00 A.M.–8:00 P.M. Thrusday, 12:00–5:00 P.M. Sunday.

Info: Renovations to the Hillman Hall of Minerals and Gems were completed in 2007. The renovations included new display cases, lighting, and specimen displays, including one that features a massive calcite that was displayed during the 1893 World's Columbian Exposition in Chicago, and new minerals from India. Additional renovations will include the creation of the Werz Gallery of Gems and Jewelry that focuses on gems, crystals, and jewelry from precious stones.

Some of the highlights at Hillman Hall of Minerals and Gems, one of the premier mineral halls in North America, include specimens from around the world, a case on pseudomorphs, a case on quartz, a case on twins, a fluorescent mineral display, minerals from the former Soviet Union and a collection of Pennsylvania specimens, including many from mines that quit producing over 100 years ago. A "float" copper exhibit allows hands-on investigations.

Admission: Adults $15.00, seniors $12.00 and children 3–18 $11.00, under 3 free.

Directions: The Carnegie Museum is located inside the city limits of Pittsburgh, on Forbes Avenue in the Oakland section of the city. From the north or west, take I-279 to I-376. Take the Forbes Avenue exit, and stay on Forbes to the Carnegie Museum and Library complex. From the east, take I-376 to the Bates Street exit. Turn right, and stay on that street until it ends, then turn left. Take the second right, and follow that road to the Carnegie Museum and Library complex.

SCRANTON

Museums/Mine Tour

Anthracite Museum Complex
RR #1, Bald Mountain Road
McDade Park
Scranton, PA 18504
Phone: (570) 963-4804
Fax: (570) 963-4194
www.anthracitemuseum.org

Info: Several mining or mining-related attractions are found at or near McDade Park, a reclaimed strip mine in Scranton, Pennsylvania. Some attractions are free; others have admission fees.

Lackawanna Coal Mine Tour: Guided tour 300 feet deep into an anthracite coal mine. See how the "black diamonds" were "harvested" from the earth. Mine temperature is 55°F, so jackets or sweatshirts may be needed. Site also has a gift shop and snack bar. Open April–November, 10:00 A.M.– 4:30 P.M. (800) 238-7245. Admission: Adults $6.00, children 3–12 $4.00, seniors 65 and over $5.75. Located at McDade Park; take Keyser Avenue exit off the Scranton Expressway, travel 3 miles, and turn right at the sign.

Pennsylvania Anthracite Heritage Museum: Explore the history and heritage of the people who settled the anthracite region. Site also has a research library and a store. Open all year Monday–Saturday 9:00 A.M.–5:00 P.M., Sunday noon–5:00 P.M. Call for winter schedule; closed Mondays in December, January, February and March. (570) 963-4804. Admission: Adults $4.00, children 6–17 $2.00, seniors over 60 $3.50. Located at McDade Park; take Keyser Avenue exit off the Scranton Expressway, travel 3 miles, and turn right at the sign.

Scranton Iron Furnaces: Four stone blast furnace stacks symbolize Scranton's industrial heritage. At one time these furnaces were the second largest producers of iron in the nation, and they produced one sixth of the nation's rail output. Tours and events are offered. Open seasonally. (570) 963-4804. Free. Take exit 185 off I-81, Central Scranton Expressway, to site.

Everhart Museum: Northwestern Pennsylvania's leading museum of natural history. The museum has a variety of exhibits and educational programs on minerals. Open all year daily, 10:00 A.M.–5:00 P.M. (570) 346-7186. Located in Nay Aug Park. Take exit 185 (Central Scranton) off I-81 and follow signs to Jefferson Avenue. Turn right onto Mulberry Street, and go straight to Nay Aug Park.

Other related sites:
▪ Museum of Anthracite Mining: Located in Ashland; see listing for Ashland.

• Eckley Mining Village: Located in Hazelton; commemorates the history and heritage of the anthracite coal miners.

TARENTUM

Museum/Mine Tour

Tour-Ed Mine
748 Bull Creek Road
Tarentum, PA 15084
Phone: (724) 224-4720
E-mail: info@tour-edmine.com
www.tour-edmine.com

Open: Memorial Day–Labor Day, daily (except Tuesday) 10:00 A.M.–4:00 P.M. Last tour at 3:20 P.M.

Info: Take an underground tour of a bituminous coal mine. Begin the tour by learning of past and present safety equipment, then board a mantrip car for your journey into the mine. Leave the car and follow your guide to learn about mining methods and machines. After the demonstrations, reboard the car, and return outside. Outside, view displays of surface mining equipment, see a working sawmill, and view a restored 1780s log cabin. The museum contains thousands of items showing what life was like in an early 1900s mining community.

Admission: Adults $8.00, children 12 and under $6.50, group rates available.

Other services available: Gift shop.

Directions: Located at exit 14 (Tarentum) on Route 28 north from Pittsburgh; 25 minutes from downtown Pittsburgh. From the PA Turnpike, take State Highway 910 to State Highway 28.

UNIONTOWN

Museum

The Coal and Coke Heritage Center
Penn State Fayette, The Eberly Campus
One University Drive
P.O. Box 519
Uniontown, PA 15401
Phone: (724) 430-4158
Fax: (724) 430-4152
E-mail: pxs47@psu.edu
www.coalandcokepsu.org

Open: 10:00 A.M.–3:00 P.M. Monday–Friday and by appointment.

Info: The Coal and Coke Heritage Center captures and preserves the history and heritage of the Connellsville Coke Region during the 100-year span from 1870 to 1970. Located at the base of Chestnut Ridge in SW Pennsylvania, the Connellsville Coke Region is famous for the abundant, high-quality bituminous coal and the coke industries that resulted. During this period of phenomenal industrial growth in the U.S., the Region fueled the blast furnaces of the Pittsburgh steel industry. The collections held by the Center include mining and coking artifacts, literature, photographs, maps, blueprints, documents, and newspapers. Exhibits feature displays highlighting coals, coke, and communities.

Admission: Donations are appreciated.

Other services available: Lectures, tours, and a speaker's bureau.

Directions: The Center is located on the lower level of the campus library. The campus is located on US Route 119, 5 miles north of Uniontown, and 7 miles south of Connellsville.

WAYNESBURG

Museum

The Paul R. Stewart Museum
Waynesburg University
51 College Street
Waynesburg, PA 15370-9987
Phone: (724) 852-3214
www.waynesburg.edu/depts/museum

Open: Monday–Friday 9:00 A.M.–noon during the school year. Special tours and summer hours by appointment.

Info: The museum has an outstanding mineral collection, with specimens from around the world. The museum was started in the 1920s by Prof. A. J. Waychoff, who would send back specimens from his travels. In addition, Prof. Waychoff collected many others locally. Other specimens were obtained as donations from alumni stationed all over the world during World War I and World War II.

Paul P. Stewart, Waychoff's nephew, continued the collection when he served as president of the college for 42 years. Some specimens are from a geology field station Stewart set up in Colorado. His will named James "Fuzzy" Randolph, who had been helping with the museum, as curator. Prof. Randolph is always willing to share the many interesting facts and stories behind the collection of the Paul R. Stewart Museum.

The museum is one of the showcases of the Waynesburg College Campus today and could boast of having one of the finest college collections of geological specimens and Indian artifacts in the country. The fossil collection includes Permian flora from local coal mines. The museum collections also include early American glass and a great collection of salt glazed stoneware from early local factories. The collections are available for scholarly study.

Admission: Free.

Directions: Waynesburg is located on I-79, just north of the Pennsylvania–West Virginia border. Take exit 3 off I-79, and turn right onto State Highway 21 at the end of the ramp. Follow Highway 21 to the third traffic light, and turn right. Follow this road into town. At the fifth traffic light after the turn, turn right again (at the courthouse) onto Washington Street. Go two blocks to Miller Hall, which is the large red brick building on the left in the third block. Turn left into College Street in front of Miller Hall, go to the end of the block, and turn right onto Morris Street, then turn right into the parking lot. The museum is in Miller Hall.

WEST CHESTER

Museum

Geology Museum
West Chester University
Department of Geology and Astronomy
Boucher 207
West Chester, PA 19383-2150
Phone: (610) 436-2727
http://www.wcupa.edu
(type "geology" under keyword search)

Open: During school sessions.
Info: The museum has collections from several noted collectors. One collection focuses on specimens from Chester County, and another highlights fluorescent minerals.
Admission: Free.
Directions: On the campus of West Chester University, in the Schmucker Science Center II.

WILKES-BARRE

Museum

Luzerne County Historical Society
69 South Franklin Street
Wilkes-Barre, PA 18701
Phone: (570) 823-1727
Fax: (570) 823-9011
E-mail: museum@luzernecountyhistory
.com

Open: *Note:* The anthracite coal exhibit is currently closed for renovations. Call for reopening info.

Info: The museum has a display on anthracite coal mining, which includes a timbered coal mine gangway and its mine railway car.
Admission: Free; donations appreciated.
Other services available: Gift shop.
Directions: On South Franklin Street in the city of Wilkes-Barre.

WINDBER

Museum

Windber Coal Heritage Center
501 15th Street
P.O. Box 115
Windber, PA 15963-0115
Phone: (814) 467-6680

Open: By appointment only.
Info: Housed in an old coal company headquarters building and featuring the mine rescue exhibit Quecreek, the Center uses high-tech exhibits, media presentations and archives to describe the everyday life of the coal miner and his family, the evolution of mining techniques, unionization, and the impact of the coal industry on small mining towns such as Windber.
Admission: Call for rates.
Directions: The Center is located at the corner of 15th Street and Graham Avenue (Route 160) in Windber, next to the Miner's Park.

Ringing Rocks

There are two locations in Eastern Pennsylvania where there are boulder fields of rocks, many of which ring with a tone when struck with a hammer or another rock. One is Ringing Rocks Park, Ringing Rock Rd., Upper Black Eddy, PA 18972 (Bucks County), the other is Ringing Hill Fire Company Park, on North Charlotte Street, (PA Rte 663), in Lower Pottsgrove Township, Montgomery County.

In June of 1890, Dr. J. J. Ott held the first-ever rock concert when he collected a number of rocks with different pitches then, accompanied by a brass band, played several musical selections for the Buckwampum Historical Society. The tones are thought to occur due to high iron content in the mineral that makes up the boulders. The only other occurrence of ringing rocks in the U.S. is on Bureau of Land Management lands between Butte and Whitehall, MT.

SECTION 3: Special Events and Tourist Information

TOURIST INFORMATION

State Tourist Agency

Pennsylvania Tourism Office
400 North Street
4th Floor
Harrisburg, PA 17120-0225
Phone: (717) 787-5453; (800) VISITPA
or (800) 847-4872
Fax: (717) 787-0687
www.visitpa.com

RHODE ISLAND

State Mineral: Bowenite
State Stone/Rock: Cumberlandite

SECTION 1: Fee Dig Sites and Guide Services

No information available.

SECTION 2: Museums and Mine Tours

PROVIDENCE

Museum

Museum of Natural History and
Planetarium
Roger Williams Park
1000 Elmwood Avenue
Providence, RI 02907
Phone: (401) 785-9450, ext. 221;
weekends and evenings:
(401) 785-9457, ext. 221
www.providenceri.com/museum/
Open: 10:00 A.M.–5:00 P.M. daily.
Info: Rhode Island's only natural history
museum has collections of minerals,
rocks, and fossils, assembled primarily by
local collectors from around the world.
Admission: Adults $2.00, children
under 8 $1.00.
Directions: From I-95 south, take exit
17, turn left at light, then turn left into
Roger Williams Park and follow signs to
the museum.

From I-95 North, take exit 16, bear
right, then turn left at the light onto
Elmwood Avenue. Turn right into Roger
Williams Park, and follow signs to the
museum.

SECTION 3: Special Events and Tourist Information

TOURIST INFORMATION

State Tourist Agency

Rhode Island Tourism Division
315 Iron Horse Way, Ste. 101
Providence, RI 02903

Phone: (800) 556-2484
Fax: (401) 273-8270
www.visitrhodeisland.com

VERMONT

Barre

Norwich

Proctor

Ludlow

State Gemstone: Grossular Garnet
State Mineral: Talc
State Stone/Rock: Granite, Marble, Slate

SECTION 1: Fee Dig Sites and Guide Services

LUDLOW / *Native • Easy*

Pan for Gold *T*

The following gems or minerals may be found:

• Gold

Camp Plymouth State Park
2008 Scout Camp Road
Ludlow, VT 05149
Phone: (802) 228-2025

Open: Memorial Day–Labor Day.
Info: Buffalo Brook, which flows through the park, was the site of the Vermont gold rush, which lasted approximately 30 years. The site was a Boy Scout camp until it became a State Park in 1984.
Rates: Call for rates and reservations.
Other services available: Camping, recreational facilities. No pets are allowed in the Park.
Directions: From Highway 100 in Tyson: cross the concrete bridge, go 1 mile east uphill to crossroad and turn left, go 1 mile north on the east side of Echo Lake.

Vermont Gold Rush

In 1855, gold was discovered in the gravel of Buffalo Brook in Plymouth, Vermont. The brook soon got the name "Gold Brook" and had claims all along its length. Several mines were started, and a stamp mill was constructed to process gold ore. However, the gold rush was short lived, and had died out by the late 1880s.

SECTION 2: Museums and Mine Tours

BARRE

Quarry Tour

Rock of Ages Corporation
P.O. Box 482
Barre, VT 05641-0482
Visitors' Center Phone: (802) 476-3119
Fax: (802) 476-0329
www.rockofages.com

Open: Visitors' Center open May 1–October 31, 8:30 A.M.–5:00 P.M. Monday–Saturday, 10:00 A.M.–5:00 P.M. Sunday. Closed July 4. 8:30 A.M.–5:00 P.M. Sunday mid-September–mid-October.

Manufacturing facility tour open almost all year, Monday–Friday, 8:00 A.M.–3:30 P.M.

Upper E. L. Smith Quarry tour June–mid-October, 9:15 A.M.–3:35 P.M.

Monday–Saturday; 10.15 A.M.–3:35 P.M. Sunday.

Info: Watch granite being quarried, and view finished products being made. Watch videos on granite quarrying at the visitors center. Pick out a free granite sample from the grout box. Learn to sandblast your own granite souvenir. For a charge, take a narrated tour of the deepest granite quarry in the world. The visitors' center also displays mineral exhibits and geological information, and has a gift shop. There is also a small picnic area and a shop selling sandwiches and Vermont products, including maple syrup.

Manufacturing facility tour: Admission free.

Upper E. L. Smith tour charges: Adults $4.50, seniors $4.00, children 6–12 $2.00, children under 6 free.

Directions: Take Highway 63 (Exit 6) from I-89. Cross Highway 14 and continue up Middle Hill Road. Follow signs to the visitors center.

NORWICH

Museum

Montshire Museum of Science
One Montshire Road
Norwich, VT 05055
Phone: (802) 649-2200
Fax: (802) 649-3637
E-mail: montshire@montshire.net
www.montshire.net

Open: All year, daily 10:00 A.M.–5:00 P.M. except Thanksgiving, Christmas, and New Year's Day.

Info: The museum has a limited display of fluorescent minerals.

Admission: Adults $7.50, children 3–17 $6.50, children under 3 free.

Directions: Norwich is located at exit 13 on I-91, just north of White River Junction.

PROCTOR

Mine Tour

Vermont Marble Museum
52 Main Street
P.O. Box 607
Proctor, VT 05767
Phone: (800) 427-1396; (802) 459-2948
www.vermont-marble.com

Open: Open 7 days/week, mid-May–mid-November. Call for times.

Info: A theater presents "The Legacy of Vermont Marble," a film showing how marble was formed over 400 million years ago. See the step-by-step process of marble quarrying. Watch a sculptor working.

Tour the Gallery of Presidents: life-sized white marble bas-relief busts of each of the past presidents. Tour the open-air marble market. View the exhibit "Earth Alive" and experience earth's geological history and its ongoing evolution.

Admission: Call for prices.

Directions: Take exit 6 from U.S. 4 in West Rutland. Turn east on Business Route 4 and then north on Vermont Route 3 to Proctor. Turn left over the marble bridge and bear right to the exhibit.

From the north, bear right on Vermont Route 3 from U.S. 7 in Pittsford to Proctor.

SECTION 3: Special Events and Tourist Information

TOURIST INFORMATION

State Tourist Agency 🖎

Vermont Department of Tourism and
Marketing
National Life Building, 6th Fl.
Drawer 20
Montpelier, VT 05620
Phone: (800) VERMONT;
(800) 837-6668; (802) 828-3237
E-mail: info@vermontvacation.com
www.1-800-vermont.com/

WISCONSIN

State Mineral: Galena (1971)
State Stone/Rock: Red Granite (1971)

No information available.

SECTION 2: Museums and Mine Tours

DODGEVILLE

Museum

The Museum of Minerals and Crystals
4228 State Road 23
Dodgeville, WI 53533-9801
Phone: (608) 935-5205

Open: April 1–Memorial Day, 9:00 A.M.–4:00 P.M. Memorial Day weekend–Labor Day weekend 9:00 A.M.–5:00 P.M., after Labor Day–October 31, 9:00 A.M.–4:00 P.M., closed Sundays.

Info: The museum contains thousands of geological specimens from around the world. Highlights of the collection include a 215-pound amethyst-filled geode, a 315-pound Brazilian agate, and a single 90-pound quartz crystal from Arkansas. The museum also has local specimens, a black light exhibit of fluorescent minerals, and a display of faceted lead crystals.

Admission: Adults $5.00, students $4.00.

Other services: Gift shop.

Directions: Located on State Highway 23, 4 miles north of Dodgeville, across from the entrance to Governor Dodge State Park, 5 miles south of House on the Rock.

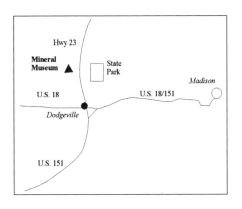

HURLEY

Museum/Mine Exhibit

Iron County Historical Museum
303 Iron Street
Hurley, WI 54534
Phone: (715) 561-2244
www.hurleywi.com/historymuseum1.aspx

Open: Monday, Wednesday, Friday, and Saturday 9:00 A.M.–1:00 P.M.

Info: This museum has exhibits on the area's mining history. Displays include iron ore and other local mineral samples.

Admission: Free. Group tours, $25.00.

Directions: At the corner of Iron Street and 3rd Avenue in Hurley.

For a nearby related display, visit: Plummer Mine Interpretive Park

Located on State Highway 77 southwest from Hurley. This is the last remaining mine head frame in Wisconsin and is surrounded by an interpretive park that honors the area's miners.

MADISON

Museum 🏛

Geology Museum
Weeks Hall
University of Wisconsin–Madison
1215 West Dayton Street
Madison, WI 53706
Phone: (608) 262-2399
Fax: (608) 262-0693
www.geologywisc.edu/~museum/

Open: All year except major holidays, Monday–Friday 8:30 A.M.–4:30 P.M.,

Saturday 9:00 A.M.–1:00 P.M.

Info: This museum has a mineral collection, which includes a display of fluorescent minerals, meteorites, and a walk-through model of a Wisconsin cave.

Note: Website contains a discussion on how to identify meteorites.

Admission: Free.

Directions: In Weeks Hall on the college campus, at the corner of Charter and Dayton Streets. Note that on-street parking is extremely limited; however, most university parking lots in the vicinity are available on non-football Saturdays.

MENASHA

Museum 🏛

Weis Earth Science Museum
University of Wisconsin, Fox Valley
1478 Midway Road
Menasha, WI 54952
Phone: (920) 832-2925 or (920) 832-2868
http://www.uwfox.uwc.edu/wesm/

Open: Wednesday–Thursday, noon–4:00 P.M.; Friday, noon-7:00 P.M.; Saturday, 10:00 A.M.–5:00 P.M.; Sunday, 1:00 P.M–5:00 P.M.; closed Mondays, Tuesdays, and all campus holidays.

Info: The Weis Earth Science Museum is the official State Mineralogical Museum of Wisconsin. It is dedicated to the geology and mineral and mining heritage of Wisconsin.

Rates: Adults $2.00, seniors 65+ and children 13–17 $1.50, children 3–12 $1.00.

Other services available: Gift shop; group tours and summer camps are also available.

Directions: In Menasha, at the intersections of Highways 47, 441, and 10. Check the website or call for detailed directions.

MILWAUKEE

Museum

Milwaukee Public Museum
800 West Wells Street
Milwaukee, WI 53233
Phone: (414) 278-2702
www.mpm.edu

Open: All year except major holidays, 9:00 A.M.–5:00 P.M. Monday–Saturday; noon–5:00 P.M., Sunday.

Info: The museum displays some of its over half a million geological specimens from around the world.

Admission: Adults $11.00, seniors (62+) $9.00, and children $7.00. Children

under 2 free.

Other services available: Gift shop, theater, restaurant.

Directions: In downtown Milwaukee, take the West Wells Street/U.S. 18 exit off I-43, and drive 1½ blocks east. The museum is on the left.

PLATTEVILLE

Museum/Mine Tour

The Mining Museum
The 1845 Bevans Lead Mine
City of Platteville, Museum Department
405 E. Main, P.O. Box 780
Platteville, WI 53818-0780
Phone: (608) 348-3301
www.mining.jamison.museum/index.html

Open: May–October 9:00 A.M.–5:00 P.M., 7 days/week. November–April 9:00 A.M.–4:00 P.M. self-guided exhibits open.Closed major holidays. Group tours year around by appointment.

Info: The mining museum traces the development of lead and zinc mining in

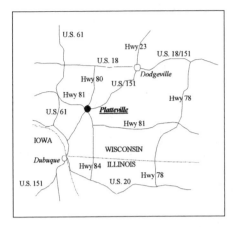

The tour of the museum, the mine, and the train ride, along with a second museum tour (Rollo Jamison Museum displaying turn-of-the-century items), take approximately 1½ hours. Comfortable shoes and a light jacket are suggested. Rides on the mine train are included if weather permits.

Admission: Adults $8.00, children 5–15 $3.00, seniors 65+ $7.00.

Directions: Platteville is located at the intersection of Highway 80 and U.S. 151.

POTOSI

Mine Tour 🏛

St. John Mine
129 S. Main Street
Potosi, WI 53820
Phone: (608) 763-2121
www.grantcounty.org/ci/potositennyson

Open: May 1–October 31 daily, 9:00 A.M.–5:00 P.M.

the upper Mississippi valley through models, dioramas, artifacts, and photographs. A guided tour includes a walk down into the Bevans Lead, an 1845 lead mine, which produced over 2 million pounds of lead ore in one year. It also includes a visit to a mine head frame where you can see how zinc ore was hoisted from a mine and hand sorted. A train ride around the museum grounds in ore cars pulled by a 1931 mine locomotive is also available.

> The southwestern Wisconsin region had surface deposits of lead, zinc, and copper ore which were mined for centuries before European settlement. In the 1830s, however, a lead-mining craze brought miners flooding in, and the region boomed. By the 1830s, news of the "rush" had reached England, and miners from Cornwall and other regions immigrated and started digging deep mines in search of ore. In the late 1840s as the easy ores were dwindling, the news of the California Gold Rush drew many miners west, and the lead rush subsided. In the later part of the 1800s however, it was discovered that the waste material discarded during lead mining was a rich zinc ore, and zinc production boomed in the area, peaking in 1917 and ending in 1971.

Info: This mine was a natural cave, which had veins of rich lead ore worked by the Native Americans as early as the 1600s. Shown to a French explorer in 1690, the mine was worked as needed by local French settlers. A peace treaty signed in 1827 opened the area to settlers, more intensive mining began, and a mining village grew around the mine. The mine closed in the 1870s.

Rates: Call for rates.

Directions: Call for specific directions.

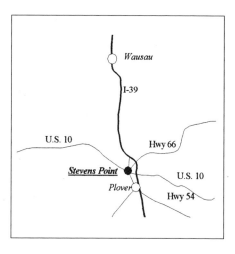

STEVENS POINT

Museum

Museum of Natural History
University of Wisconsin–Stevens Point
900 Reserve Road
Stevens Point, WI 54481
Phone: (715) 346-2858
http://www.uwsp.edu/museum/

Open: During regular semester hours: Sunday 1:00–4:00 P.M., Monday 9:00 A.M.–7:00 P.M., Tuesday–Friday 9:00 A.M.–4:00 P.M., Saturday 10:00 A.M.–3:00 P.M. Summer: Monday–Friday 9:00 A.M.–4:00 P.M., closed Saturday and Sunday.

Info: 150 rocks and minerals are on display. Displays show how minerals form and evolve.

Admission: Free; donations appreciated.

Directions: Located on the University of Wisconsin–Stevens Point campus, at the intersection of Reserve Road and Portage Street.

SECTION 3: Special Events and Tourist Information

ANNUAL EVENT

Agate Days

Info: Agate Days is held in July at the University of Wisconsin, Fox Valley, and is sponsored by the Weis Earth Science Museum. The event includes educational presentations, displays of agate specimens, family activities, a silent auction, and dealers.

ANNUAL EVENT

Quarry Quest

Info: Quarry Quest is a one-day event held in September at the Michels Materials Limestone Quarry in Neenah, WI, sponsored by the Weis Earth Science Museum. It has a wide variety of family activities at the quarry. More information can be found by calling the Weis Museum, checking the Weis website or the event website, www.QuarryQuest.com. Admission is charged, with all proceeds benefiting local charities.

TOURIST INFORMATION

State Tourist Agency

Wisconsin Department of Tourism
P.O. Box 8690
Madison, WI 53707-7976
Phone: (800) 432-TRIP;
(800) 432-8747 or (608) 206-2161
E-mail: tourinfo@travelwisconsin.com
www.travelwisconsin.com

Chamber of Commerce

Hurley Area Chamber of Commerce
316 Silver Street
Hurley, WI 54534
Phone: (715) 561-4334
www.hurleywi.com

Information on Hurley's historic mining area, one of the most famous mining towns of all time.

Iron County Heritage Days are from the last week in July to mid-August.

Index by State

ALABAMA

Fee Dig Mines and Guide Services
Cragford   Alabama Gold Camp—Pan or prospect for gold

Museums and Mine Tours
Aldrich   Aldrich Coal Mine Museum—Artifacts and simulated coal mine

Anniston   Anniston Museum of Natural History—Gemstones, meteorite, artificial indoor cave

Dora   Alabama Mining Museum—Focus on coal mining

McCalla   Tannehill Ironworks Historical State Park—Geology relevant to the iron industry

Tuscaloosa   Alabama Museum of Natural History—Minerals, meteorite

ALASKA

Fee Dig Mines and Guide Services
Anchorage   Alaska DNR—Pan, prospect, excavate, limited suction dredging for gold

Chicken   Chicken Gold Camp and Outpost—Pan or dig for gold

Chugach National Forest   Chugach National Forest—Pan for gold

Copper Center   Wrangell-St. Elias National Park and Preserve—Pan for gold, hunt for rocks and minerals (see exceptions in listing)

Fairbanks   El Dorado Gold Mine—Gold panning
    Faith Creek Camp—Pan, sluice, dredge for gold
    Gold Dredge No. 8—Gold panning

Girdwood   Crow Creek Mine—Pan, dredge, or use metal detectors for gold

Juneau   Alaska Gastineau Mill and Gold Mine—Pan or dig for gold or garnets

McGrath   Moore Creek Mining, LLC—Camp and prospect or dredge for gold

Nome   Nome Beaches—Pan for gold

Skagway   Klondike Gold Dredge Tours—Pan for gold
    Liarsville Gold Rush Trail Camp and Salmon Bake—Pan for gold

Talkeetna	Clark/Wiltz Mining—Camp and prospect (with metal detectors) for gold

Museums and Mine Tours

Chicken	The Chicken Gold Camp & Outpost—Gold dredge tour
Fairbanks	El Dorado Gold Mine—Gold mine tour and gold nugget display
	Gold Dredge No. 8—Gold dredge tour
	University of Alaska Museum—Minerals and gems from Alaska, Arctic Canada, and the Pacific Rim; includes gold and meteorites
Juneau	Alaska Gastineau Mill and Gold Mine—Mine tour
	Juneau-Douglas City Museum—History of gold mining
	Last Chance Mining Museum—Hard-rock gold mining museum
Nome	The Carrie N. McLain Memorial Museum—History of area gold mining
Skagway	Klondike Gold Dredge Tour—Gold dredge tour
	Liarsville Gold Rush Trail and Salmon Bake—Tour of gold rush camp
	Klondike Gold Rush National Historic Park—History of area gold mining
Wasilla	Independence Mine State Historical Park—Guided mine tour

ARIZONA

Fee Dig Mines and Guide Services

Apache Jct.	Apache Trail Tours—Gold panning jeep tours
Glendale	William Gardner III—Guide service; collect aragonite, fluorite, chrysocolla, quartz, galena, amethyst, fluorescent minerals, smithsonite, wulfenite (in a variety of forms), willemite, calcite, barite
Goldfield	Goldfield Ghost Town, Scenic Railroad, and Mine Tours—Gold panning
Prescott	Lynx Creek Mineral Withdrawal Area, Prescott National Forest—Pan for gold
Safford	Black Hills Rockhound Area—Dig for fire agates
	Round Hill Rockhound Area—Search for fire agates, chalcedony, small geodes.
Tempe	Fat Jack Mine—Collect amethyst scepters, quartz, garnet, tourmaline, limonite
Wickenburg	Robson's Mining World—Pan for gold (open for special events only)

Museums and Mine Tours

Apache Jct.	Superstition Mountain Museum—Geology, minerals, and mining
Bisbee	Bisbee Mining and Historical Museum—Displays on local mining
	Queen Mine Tour—Tour an underground copper mine
Flagstaff	Meteor Crater Enterprises, Inc.—View a meteor crater, museum of astrogeology

	Museum of Northern Arizona—History of Colorado Plateau, geologic models, mineral specimens
Goldfield	Goldfield Ghost Town, Scenic Railroad, and Mine Tours—Gold mine tour, museum, ghost town
Morenci	Phelps Dodge Morenci Copper Mine—Tour an open-pit mine
Phoenix	Arizona Mining and Mineral Museum—3,000 minerals on exhibit including gemstones, lapidary arts, minerals from Arizona copper mines, meteorite, rock from the moon, geodes, fluorescent mineral display
Quartzsite	Quartzsite Historical Society—Displays of mining equipment
Sahuarita	ASARCO Mineral Discovery Center—Geology, mining, minerals, and tour of open-pit mine
Sun City	The Mineral Museum—3,000 rocks and minerals from the U.S. and the world, with emphasis on minerals from Arizona. Over 150 fluorescent rocks and minerals, most from Franklin and Sterling Hill, NJ
Tempe	Robert S. Dietz Museum of Geology—Mineral displays, seismograph
Tombstone	Good Enough Mine—Gold mine tour
Tucson	Arizona-Sonora Desert Museum—Mineral collection from Sonora desert region
	Flandreau: University of Arizona Science Center—2,100 of 15,000 minerals on display; Arizona minerals, meteorites, fluorescents, borate minerals
Wickenburg	Robson's Mining World—Tour old gold mining village (special events only)
	Vulture Gold Mine—Self-guided mine tour

Annual Events

Quartzsite	Gem and Mineral Shows—Mid-January–mid-February
Scottsdale	Minerals of Arizona—Symposium one day in March/April
Tucson	Gem and Mineral Shows—End of January through mid-February

ARKANSAS

Fee Dig Mines and Guide Services

Jessieville	Jim Coleman Crystal Mines and Rock Shop—Dig for quartz crystals
	Ron Coleman Mining, Inc.—Dig for quartz crystals
	Ouachita National Forest, Crystal Mt. Quartz Collecting Site—Collect quartz crystals on the ground, no digging permitted
Mt. Ida	The Crystal Seen Trading Co.—Dig quartz crystals
	Fiddler's Ridge Rock Shop and Crystal Mines—Dig for quartz crystals
	Ouachita National Forest, Crystal Vista Quartz Collecting Site—Collect quartz crystals on the ground, no digging permitted
	Sonny Stanley's Crystal Mine—Dig for quartz crystals
	Starfire Crystal Mine—Dig for quartz crystals

	Wegner Crystal Mine—Dig, sluice, or pick through tailings for quartz crystals
Murfreesboro	Crater of Diamonds State Park—Dig and screen for diamonds, amethyst, agates, barite, calcite, jasper, quartz, other gems
Pencil Bluff	Arrowhead Crystal Mine—Dig for quartz crystals
Story	Gee and Dee Crystal—Dig for quartz crystals
	Sweet Surrender Crystal Mine—Dig for quartz crystals

Museum and Mine Tours

Fayetteville	The University Museum—Quartz and other Arkansas minerals
Little Rock	Geology Learning Center—Arkansas gems, minerals, fossil fuels
Mt. Ida	Heritage House Museum of Montgomery County—Quartz and Mineral Exhibits
State University	ASU Museum—Minerals, many from Arkansas

Annual Events

| **Mt. Ida** | Quartz Crystal Festival and World Championship Dig—Second weekend in October |

CALIFORNIA

Fee Dig Mines and Guide Services

Coalinga	Benitoite Gem Mine—Hunt for benitoite and other gems and minerals
Coloma	Marshall Gold Discovery State Historic Park—Gold panning
Columbia	Hidden Treasures Gold Mine Tours—Pan for gold and garnets
Jackson	Kennedy Gold Mine—Gold panning
Jamestown	Gold Prospecting Adventures, LLC—Sluice, pan, and prospect with metal detectors for gold
Lucerne	Lake County Visitors Information Center—Rockhounding for Lake County "diamonds" or "moon tears"
Mariposa	Little Valley Inn at the Creek—Gold panning
Mesa Grande	Himalayan Tourmaline Mine, High Desert Gems and Minerals—Look for California tourmaline in mine tailings
Nevada City	Malakoff Diggins State Historical Park—Gold panning
Pala	Oceanview Mine—Hunt for tourmaline (pink, green, bicolor), smoky crystals, garnets, book mica, smoky crystals, cleavelandite, kunzite, morganite, gossanite (clear beryl), purple lepidolite, muscovite mica, aquamarine
Pine Grove	Roaring Camp Mining Co.—Pan for gold, rockhounding for quartz crystals, jade, jasper, and river rubies

Placerville   Hangtown's Gold Bug Park and Mine—Learn gold panning

Museums and Mine Tours

Allegany   Underground Gold Miners Tours and Museum—Tour an active gold mine

Angels Camp   Angels Camp Museum and Carriage House—Museum features rocks and minerals, gold stamping mill, mining equipment

Avalon   Catalina Island Museum Society, Inc.—Exhibits on mining on Catalina Island

Boron   Borax Visitors Center—Story of borax

Boron Twenty Mule Team Museum—History of area borate mining

Coloma   Marshall Gold Discovery State Historic Park—Gold mining exhibit/museum

Columbia   Hidden Treasure Gold Mine—Tour of active gold mine

Death Valley   Furnace Creek Borax Museum—Rocks and minerals, featuring borax minerals

El Cajon   Heritage of the Americas Museum—Rocks, minerals, and meteorites

Fallbrook   Fallbrook Gem & Mineral Society Museum—Features of minerals from San Diego County

Grass Valley   Empire Mine State Historic Park—Hard-rock gold mine

Independence   Eastern California Museum—Regional gem and mineral collection

Jackson   Amador County Museum—Collection of mineral spheres from California, Utah, and Nevada

Kennedy Gold Mine Tours—Surface tour of gold mine

Julian   Eagle and High Peak Gold Mine Tours—Hard-rock gold mine tour

Julian Pioneer Museum—Rock and mineral display, gold mining tools and equipment displays

Lakeport   Historic Courthouse Museum—Minerals and gems found in Lake County

Los Angeles   Natural History Museum of Los Angeles County—52,000 specimens, minerals of California, native gold, gems, and minerals

Mariposa   California State Mining and Mineral Museum—Gold from California, gems and minerals from around the world

Needles   Needles Regional Museum—Collection of Needles blue agate, Colorado River pebble terrace stones

Nevada City   Malakoff Diggins Park Association—History of hydraulic gold mining

Pacific Grove   Pacific Grove Museum of Natural History—Monterey County rocks, fluorescent minerals

Paso Robles	El Paso des Robles Area Pioneer Museum—Display of local minerals
Placerville	Hangtown's Gold Bug Park and Mine—Tour hard-rock gold mine
Quincy	Plumas County Museum—Exhibits on gold and copper mining in Plumas County
Rancho Palos Verdes	Point Vicente Interpretive Center—Exhibits on area geology
Red Bluff	Gaumer's Mineral and Mining Museum—Minerals from around the world
Redlands	San Bernardino County Museum—45,000 rocks, minerals, and gems
Ridgecrest	Maturango Museum—Small but well-rounded regional gem and mineral collection
Riverside	Jurupa Mountains Cultural Center—Crestmore minerals display, minerals from around the world on display and for sale, family education programs
	World Museum of Natural History—Fluorescent minerals, meteorites, tektites, over 1,300 mineral spheres
San Diego	San Diego Natural History Museum—26,000 mineral specimens, includes minerals found in San Diego County mines
Santa Barbara	Department of Earth Sciences, UCSB—Gem and mineral collection, minerals and their tectonic settings
Shoshone	Shoshone Museum—Rock collection reflecting the geology of the area
Sierra City	Kentucky Mine and Museum—Exhibits of local gold and mercury mining
Sonora	Tuolomne County Museum—Gold from local mines
Vallecito	Sutters Gold Mine—Hard-rock gold mine tour
Yermo	Calico Ghost Town—Explore a silver mine
Yreka	Siskiyou County Courthouse—Gold exhibit
Yucca Valley	Hi-Desert Nature Museum—Rock and mineral collection, includes fluorescent minerals

Annual Events

| **Boron** | Rock Bonanza—Weekend before Easter |
| **Coloma** | Marshall Gold Discovery State Historic Park: Gold Rush Live—End of September–beginning of October |

COLORADO

Fee Dig Mines and Guide Services

| **Breckenridge** | Country Boy Mine—Pan for gold |

Granite	Gold Basin Mine—Prospect for gold
Idaho Springs	Argo Gold Mill—Pan for gold and gemstones
	Phoenix Mine—Pan for gold
Ouray	Bachelor-Syracuse Mine Tour—Learn to pan for gold
Silverton	Old Hundred Gold Mine Tours, Inc.—Pan for gold

Museums and Mine Tours

Breckenridge	Country Boy Mine—Hard-rock gold mine tour
Central City	Gilpin History Museum—Displays of local minerals
Colorado Springs	Western Museum of Mining and Industry—Displays of mining and demonstrations on gold panning
Creede	Creede Underground Mining Museum—Displays of rocks, minerals, and mining equipment
Cripple Creek	Cripple Creek District Museum—Mineral displays
	Molly Kathleen Gold Mine—Gold mine tour
Denver	Denver Museum of Nature and Science—2,000 specimens; includes gold, topaz, aquamarine, amazonite, and other Colorado minerals
Georgetown	Lebanon Silver Mine—Ride a narrow-gauge train, then take a walking tour of the silver mine
Golden	Geology Museum, Colorado School of Mines—50,000 specimens, minerals from Colorado and from around the world, gemstones and precious metals, cave exhibit
Idaho Springs	Argo Gold Mill—Historic gold mill, mining museum, Double Eagle Gold Mine
	Edgar Experimental Mine—Tour an experimental mine (silver, gold, lead, copper)
	Phoenix Mine—See a working underground hard-rock mine (gold, silver)
Lake City	Hard Tack Mine—Gold mine tour
Lakewood	Hidee Gold Mine—Gold mine tour and gold ore sample
Leadville	Matchless Mine—Tour a symbol of the financial hazards of silver mining.
	National Mining Hall of Fame and Museum—Story of the American mining industry from coal to gold
Ouray	Bachelor-Syracuse Mine—Underground tour of gold and silver mine
	Ouray County Historical Society—Mineral and mining displays
Salida	Lost Mine Tour—Tour a closed manganese mine
Silverton	Mayflower Gold Mill—Tour a gold mill
	Old Hundred Gold Mine Tour, Inc.—Gold mine tour

San Juan County Historical Society Museum—Minerals and gems from the Silverton area

Victor   Mine View—View of Colorado's largest open-pit gold mine

CONNECTICUT

Fee Dig Mines and Guide Services

Roxbury   Green's Farm Garnet Mine—Search for garnets

Museums and Mine Tours

East Granby   Old New-Gate Prison and Copper Mine—Tour an old copper mine

Greenwich   Bruce Museum of Arts and Sciences—Exhibits of minerals and rocks

Kent   Museum of Mining and Mineral Science—Local minerals

New Haven   Peabody Museum of Natural History, Yale University—Minerals of New England and the world

DELAWARE

Fee Dig Mines and Guide Services

Wilmington   Woodlawn Quarry—Look through tailing piles for feldspar, quartz, mica, garnet, beryl

Museums and Mine Tours

Newark   Iron Hill Museum—Natural history of Delaware, rock and mineral collections

University of Delaware, Mineralogical Museum—5,000 specimens (1,000 on display), crystals, gems, minerals

DISTRICT OF COLUMBIA

Fee Dig Mines and Guide Services

None

Museums and Mine Tours

Smithsonian Institution, National Museum of Natural History—Gems and minerals (over 375,000 specimens and a research collection)

FLORIDA

Fee Dig Mines and Guide Services

Ft. Drum   Ft. Drum Crystal Mine—Collect calcite encrusted fossil shells, micropyrite, irridescent marcosite

Museums and Mine Tours

Deland   Gillespie Museum, Stetson University—Minerals, gemstones, faceting, replica mine and cave

Mulberry   Mulberry Phosphate Museum—Exhibits on the phosphate industry

Tampa   Ed and Bernadette Marcin Museum, University of Florida—Minerals and gemstones, mainly from Florida and the western U.S.

GEORGIA

Fee Dig Mines and Guide Services

Cleveland   Gold'n Gem Grubbin—Dig and pan for gold, sapphires, rubies, emeralds, amethyst, topaz

Dahlonega   Consolidated Gold Mine—Gold panning

Crisson Gold Mine—Pan gold sands or enriched gemstone ore

Gainesville Chattahoochee-Oconee National Forest—Gold panning, rockhounding (restrictions apply)

LaGrange   Hogg Mine, Dixie Euhedrals—Collect star rose quartz, aquamarine, beryl (rare), black tourmaline

LaGrange Clear Quartz Crystals, Dixie Euhedrals—Collect clear quartz crystals

Lincolnton   Graves Mountain—Search for audite, lazulite, pyrophyllite, kyanite, hematite, pyrite, ilmenite, muscovite, fuchsite, barite, sulfur, blue quartz, quartz crystals, microcrystals (such as woodhouseite), variscite, strengite, phosphosiderite, cacoxenite, crandallite (collecting allowed on special dates only)

Museums and Mine Tours

Atlanta   Fernbank Museum of Natural History—Joachim Gem Collection containing 400 cut and polished gemstones

Fernbank Science Center—Gems, carved opals, meteorites

Cartersville Tellus—2,000 specimens, gems and minerals from the state, simulated cave

Dahlonega   Consolidated Gold Mine—Mine tour

Dahlonega Courthouse Gold Museum—Tells the story of the Georgia gold rush

Elberton   Elberton Granite Museum & Exhibit—Granite quarry and products

Macon   Museum of Arts and Sciences—Display of gems and minerals

Statesboro   Georgia Southern Museum—Collection of rocks and minerals from Georgia's Highlands, Piedmont, and Coastal regions

Tallapoosa   West Georgia Museum of Tallapoosa—Small collection of local minerals

Annual Events

Dahlonega Gold Rush Days—Third weekend in October

     World Open Gold Panning Championship—Third Saturday of April

Jasper Pickens County Marble Festival—First weekend in October

HAWAII

Fee Dig Mines and Guide Services

    None

Museums and Mine Tours

**Hawaii
National Park** Thomas A. Jaggar Museum—Museum on vulcanology and seismology, tour of volcano

Hilo Lyman House Memorial Museum—Rocks, minerals, gems

IDAHO

Fee Dig Mines and Guide Services

Moscow 3-D's Panhandle Gems and Garnet Queen Mine—Guide service, star garnet screening

Spencer Spencer Opal Mine—Pick through a stockpile for fire opal, pre-arranged digging at the mine on specified dates

St. Maries Emerald Creek Garnet Area—Screen for star garnets

Museums and Mine Tours

Boise Museum of Mining and Geology—Exhibits on mining and geology

Caldwell The Glen L. and Ruth M. Evans Gem and Mineral Collection, Orma J. Smith Museum of Natural History—Extensive collection of minerals, agate, jasper, other gemstones, 2,000 cabochons

Kellogg Crystal Gold Mine—Mine tour

    Staff House Museum—Rocks, minerals, mining equipment

Pocatello Idaho Museum of Natural History—Displays of specimens from Idaho and the intermountain west

Wallace Sierra Silver Mine Tour—Mine tour

    Wallace District Mining Museum—Story of mining in northern Idaho

ILLINOIS

Fee Dig Mines and Guide Services

Hamilton Jacobs Geodes—Hunt for geodes containing calcite, barite, quartz, kaolinite

| **Roisclaire** | American Fluorite Museum—Dig for fluorite in mine ore |

Museums and Mine Tours

Carbondale	University Museum—Displays on geologic history
Chicago	The Field Museum—92-year-old exhibit
	Museum of Science and Industry—Simulated coal mine
Elmhurst	Lizzadro Museum of Lapidary Art—1,300 pieces of cut and polished gems, fluorescent rocks, a birthstone display
Rockford	Burpee Museum of Natural History—Displays of rocks, minerals, and gems
Rock Island	Augustana Fryxell Geology Museum—Rock and mineral museum
Rosiclare	The American Fluorite Museum—Story of fluorospar industry
Shirley	The Funk Gem and Mineral Museum—Gem and mineral collection
Springfield	Illinois State Museum—Gems and minerals, Illinois specimens, birthstones, fluorescent minerals, copper

INDIANA

Fee Dig Mines and Guide Services

| **Knightstown** | Yogi Bear's Jellystone Park Camping Resort—Midwestern gold prospecting |

Museums and Mine Tours

Bedford	Land of Limestone Exhibition—History of Indiana limestone industry
	Lawrence County Museum of History—Exhibit on limestone, geological specimens from Lawrence County.
Fort Wayne	Indiana Purdue University at Fort Wayne—Hallway displays of minerals, meteorites, and rocks
Indianapolis	Indiana State Museum—Indiana and regional minerals
Richmond	Joseph Moore Museum of Natural History, Earlham College—Geology exhibit from local Ordovician limestone

IOWA

Fee Dig Mines and Guide Services

(See annual event—Rocktober Geode Fest)

Museums and Mine Tours

Danville	Geode State Park—Display of geodes
Iowa City	University of Iowa—Displays on state geology
Sioux City	Sioux City Public Museum—Mineralogy exhibit

Waterloo	Grout Museum of History and Science—Displays of rocks and minerals
West Bend	Grotto of the Redemption—Grotto made of precious stones and gems
Winterset	Madison County Historical Society—Rock and mineral collection

Annual Events

| Keokuk | Rocktober Geode Fest—Three-day weekend in early October; field trips for geodes |

KANSAS

Fee Dig Mines and Guide Services

None

Museums and Mine Tours

Ashland	Pioneer Krier Museum—Mineral exhibit
Emporium	Johnston Geology Museum—Tri-state mining display, geological specimens from Kansas
Galena	Galena Mining and Historical Museum—Focus on local lead mining and smelting industry
Greensburg	Pallasite Meteorite at the Big Well Museum—Meteorite strike site and 1,000-pound meteorite
Hays	Sternberg Museum of Natural History—Displays of gems and minerals
Hutchinson	Kansas Underground Salt Museum and Mine Tour—Explains the underground mining of rock salt
McPherson	McPherson Museum—Meteorites

KENTUCKY

Fee Dig Mines and Guide Services

| Marion | The Ben E. Clement Mineral Museum—Fluorite and fluorescent mineral collecting |

Museums and Mine Tours

Benham	Kentucky Coal Mine Museum—Displays on coal mining and formation of coal
Covington	Behringer-Crawford Museum—Display of gems and minerals
Danville	JFC Museum—Display of gems and minerals
Lexington	Headley-Whitney Museum—Display of gems and minerals
Lynch	Lynch Portal #31 Walking Tour—Walking tour of coal mining facilities
Marion	The Ben E. Clement Mineral Museum—Display of gems and minerals
Olive Hill	Northeastern Kentucky Museum—Displays of gems and minerals

LOUISIANA

Fee Dig Mines and Guide Services
    None

Museums and Mine Tours
Shreveport   Louisiana State Exhibit Museum—Displays on mining and salt domes

MAINE

Fee Dig Mines and Guide Services
Auburn   City of Auburn/Feldspar and Greenlaw Quarries—Hunt for apatite, tourmaline, and quartz

Mt. Apatite Farm/Turner Quarry—Hunt for tourmaline, garnet, graphic granite, clevelandite, autenite, mica, beryl

Bethel   Maine Mineralogy Expeditions-Bumpus Quarry—Collect albite, almandine garnet, beryl, rose, and other quartz, black tourmaline, biotite, autunite, zircon

Songo Pond Mine—Collect tourmaline and other Maine gems and minerals

Poland   Poland Mining Camp—Collect tourmaline and other Maine gems and minerals

West Paris   Perham's of West Paris—Collect tourmaline and other Maine gems and minerals

Museums and Mine Tours
Augusta   Maine State Museum—Gems and minerals of Maine

Bethel   Maine Mineral Museum/Mt. Marin Jeweler's Gallery—Examples of gems from local and worldwide sources, crystal cave for kids

Caribou   Nylander Museum—Minerals of Maine

Presque Isle   Northern Maine Museum of Science—Display of Maine minerals, fluorescent minerals, Maine slate

West Paris   Perham's of West Paris—Maine gems and minerals, model of a feldspar quarry, model of a gem tourmaline pocket, fluorescent minerals

Annual Events
Augusta   Maine Mineral Symposium—Second full weekend in May

Poland   Maine Pegmatite Workshop—Week-long program at the end of May or beginning of June

MARYLAND

Fee Dig Mines and Guide Services
> None

Museums and Mine Tours
Kensington   Great Falls Tavern Visitor's Center—Gold Mine Trail tours scheduled periodically

MASSACHUSETTS

Fee Dig Mines and Guide Services
> None

Museums and Mine Tours
Cambridge   Harvard Museum of Natural History—Gems, minerals, ores, meteorites

Springfield   Springfield Science Museum—Minerals from around the world

MICHIGAN

Fee Dig Mines and Guide Services
Grand Marais   Woodland Park Campground—Search beaches for agates

Mohawk   Delaware Copper Mine—Search for souvenir copper

Ontonagon   Caledonia Copper Mine—Collect copper specimens, silver, epidote, calcite, datolite, quartz

Museums and Mine Tours
Ann Arbor   Exhibit Museum of Natural History, University of Michigan—Exhibits of rocks and minerals

Bloomfield Hills   Cranbrook Institute of Science—5,000 minerals and crystals from around the world (including hiddenite), gold

Calumet   Coppertown, U.S.A.—Exhibits on copper mining

Caspian   Iron County Museum and Park—Iron mining complex

Chelsea   Gerald E. Eddy Discovery Center—Michigan rocks, minerals, crystals, and mining

Copper Harbor   Fort Wilkins Historic State Park—History of copper mining in the area

Greenland   Adventure Copper Mine—Tour underground copper mine

Hancock   The Quincy Mine Hoist Association—Tour an underground copper mine

Houghton   The A. E. Seaman Mineral Museum—Crystal collection, minerals from the Lake Superior copper district

Iron Mountain	Iron Mountain Iron Mine—Iron mine tour
Lake Linden	Houghton County Historical Museum—Copper mining and refining equipment displays
Mohawk	Delaware Copper Mine—Mine tour
Mt. Pleasant	The Museum of Cultural and Natural History, Central Michigan University—Michigan rocks and minerals
Negaunee	Michigan Iron Industry Museum—Story of Michigan iron industry
Shelby	Shelby Man-Made Gemstones—Visit a gemstone factory

Annual Event

Houghton	Copper County Mineral Retreat—One week in early August, sponsored by the A. E. Seaman Museum of Michigan Tech.

MINNESOTA

Fee Dig Mines and Guide Services

> None

Museums and Mine Tours

Calumet	Hill Annex Mine State Park—Tour an open-pit iron mine
Chisholm	Ironworld Development Corporation—Iron industry taconite mining tours
	The Minnesota Museum of Mining—Indoor and outdoor exhibits
	Taconite Mine Tours—Tour of an open-pit iron ore mine
Hibbing	Mahoning Hull-Rust Mine—Observe an open-pit iron mine
Moose Lake	Minnesota Agate and Geologic Interpretive Center—Showcases Minnesota's gemstone, the Lake Superior Agate
Pipestone	Pipestone National Monument—Tour a Native American pipestone quarry
Soudan	Soudan Underground Mine State Park—Tour an underground iron mine
Virginia	Mineview in the Sky—View an open-pit iron ore mine
	Iron Range Tourism Bureau—Information on mine view sites

Annual Event

Moose Lake	Agate Days—One weekend in July

MISSISSIPPI

Fee Dig Mines and Guide Services

> None

Museums and Mine Tours

Starkville   Dunn-Seiler Museum—Mineral and rock collections

MISSOURI

Fee Dig Mines and Guide Services

Alexandria   Sheffler Rock Shop—Dig geodes lined with crystals

Museums and Mine Tours

Golden   Golden Pioneer Museum—Large mineral exhibit

Joplin   Everett J. Richie Tri-State Mineral Wing—Story of area's lead and zinc mining

Kansas City   University of Missouri, Kansas City, Geosciences Museum—Local and regional specimens

Park Hills   Missouri Mines State Historic Site—1,100 minerals, ores, and rocks

Point Lookout   Ralph Foster Museum, College of the Ozarks—Gemstone spheres and fluorescent minerals

Rolla   Mineral Museum, University of Missouri, Rolla—3,500 minerals, ores, and rocks from 92 countries and 47 states

MONTANA

Fee Dig Mines and Guide Services

Alder   Red Rock Mine and Garnet Gallery—Screen for garnets

Clinton   L-Diamond-E Ranch—Sapphire mining pack trips

Dillon   Crystal Park Recreational Mineral Collecting Area—Dig for quartz and amethyst crystal

Hamilton   Sapphire Studio—Purchase and wash bags of ore for sapphires

Helena   Spokane Bar Sapphire Mine and Gold Fever Rock Shop—Dig and screen for sapphires and other gems and minerals

Libby   Libby Creek Recreational Gold Panning Area—Pan for gold

Phillipsburg   Gem Mountain—Search for sapphires

Sapphire Country Cabin—Pan or dig for sapphires and gold

Sapphire Gallery—Wash bags of gravel to look for sapphires

Museums and Mine Tours

Butte   Anselmo Mine Yard—Tour of mining facilities and history of area mining

The Berkeley Pit—Observation point for closed open-pit copper mine

Butte-Silver Bow Visitors and Transportation Center—Presents information on area geology and its mining, including local gold and silver mining

	Mineral Museum, Montana College of Mineral Science and Technology—Gold, fluorescent minerals, and minerals from Butte and MT
	World Museum of Mining and 1899 Mining Camp—Tour of surface facilities of former silver and zinc mine
Ekalaka	Carter County Museum—Fluorescent mineral display
Lewistown	Central Montana Museum—Rocks, minerals, and Yogo sapphires

NEBRASKA

Fee Dig Mines and Guide Services
None

Museums and Mine Tours
Chadron	Eleanor Barbour Cook Museum of Geoscience—Displays of rocks and minerals
Crawford	Trailside Museum—Displays of western Nebraska geology
Hastings	Hastings Museum of Natural and Cultural History—Minerals, rocks, fluorescent minerals, and translucent slabs
Lincoln	University of Nebraska State Museum—Displays of rocks, minerals, and fluorescent rocks

NEVADA

Fee Dig Mines and Guide Services
Denio	Bonanza Opal Mines, Inc.—Dig crystal, white and black fire opal
	The Opal Queen Mining Company—Dig for crystal, white and black fire opal
	Rainbow Ridge Opal Mine—Tailings digging for wood opal
	Royal Peacock Opal Mine, Inc.—Dig black and fire opal
Ely	Garnet Fields Rockhound Area—Hunt for almandine garnets
Reno	High Desert Gems and Minerals—Gem mine tours

Museums and Mine Tours
Elko	Barrick Goldstrike Mines, Inc.—Tour an active gold mine
Las Vegas	Nevada State Museum and Historical Society—Natural history of Nevada
Nelson	Eldorado Canyon Mine Tours, Inc.—Hard-rock gold mine tour
Reno	W. M. Keck Earth Science and Mineral Engineering Museum—Collection of minerals and ores
Virginia City	Chollar Mine—Underground mine tour (gold and silver)

NEW HAMPSHIRE

Fee Dig Mines and Guide Services
Grafton   Ruggles Mine—Collect up to 150 different minerals
Laconia   Deer Hill Mineral Site—Collect amethyst, quartz, and mica
                 Moat Mountain Smokey Quartz Collecting Site—Collect quartz

Museums and Mine Tours
Contoocook   The Little Nature Museum—Rocks, minerals, and gems
Dover   The Woodman Institute—1,300 specimens including local rocks

NEW JERSEY

Fee Dig Mines and Guide Services
Cape May   Cape May Welcome Center—Hunt for Cape May "diamonds"
Franklin   Franklin Mineral Museum and Buckwheat Dump—Tailings diggings
                 for fluorescent minerals and franklinite
Ogdensburg   Sterling Hill Mine and Museum—Collect fluorescent minerals

Museum and Mine Tours
Franklin   Franklin Mineral Museum—Minerals, rocks, local and worldwide flu-
                 orescent minerals
**Monroe
Township**   Displayworld's Stone Museum—Minerals, hands-on exhibits
Morristown   The Morris Museum—Specimens from five continents
New Brunswick Rutgers Geology Museum—Specimens from the zinc deposit at
                 Franklin and the zeolite deposits from Paterson, meteorites
Ogdensburg   Sterling Hill Mine and Museum—Tour old zinc mine
Paterson   The Paterson Museum—Specimens from local basalt flows and basalt
                 flow in the Poona region of India, minerals from NJ and around the
                 world
Rutherford   Meadowland Museum—Fluorescent minerals, quartz, minerals from NJ
Trenton   New Jersey State Museum—Minerals and rocks, including fluores-
                 cents and magnetite ore

NEW MEXICO

Fee Dig Mines and Guide Services
Bingham   Blanchard Rock Shop—Collect over 84 different kinds of minerals
                 in a former lead mine
Deming   Rockhound State Park—Collect a variety of semiprecious stones
Dixon   Harding Mine—Harding pegmatite has yielded over 50 minerals

Gila	Casitas de Gila Guesthouses—Rockhound on 60 acres. Some of the minerals found are white and pink chalcedony, chalcedony roses, red, brown, and yellow jasper, jasper breccia, picture jasper, banded agate, zeolites, geodes, massive hematite, banded rhyolite, andesite, volcanic bombs, scoria, limonite and hematite-banded welded tuff. Pan for gold in the creek.
Magdalena	Bill's Gems & Minerals—Collect copper and iron minerals at mine dumps

Museums and Mine Tours

Albuquerque	Geology Museum, University of New Mexico—Displays of N.M. minerals and geology
	Institute of Meteoritics, University of New Mexico—Meteorites
	New Mexico Museum of Natural History and Science—3,000 specimens with a focus on N.M. and the southwestern U.S.
	The Turquoise Museum—Displays of turquoise
Grants	New Mexico Mining Museum—Uranium mining
Portales	Miles Mineral Museum—Displays of minerals, gems, and meteorites
Socorro	Mineralogical Museum, New Mexico Tech.—10,000 specimens of minerals from N.M., the U.S., and the world

Annual Events

Socorro	New Mexico Mineral Symposium—Two days in November

NEW YORK

Fee Dig Mines and Guide Services

Herkimer	Herkimer Diamond Mine and KOA Kampground—Dig for Herkimer "diamonds"
Middleville	Ace of Diamonds Mine and Campground—Prospect for Herkimer "diamonds," calcite crystals, and dolomite crystals
North River	The Barton Mine—Hunt for garnets
St. Johnsville	Crystal Grove Diamond Mine and Campground—Dig for Herkimer "diamonds"

Museums and Mine Tours

Albany	New York State Museum—Minerals from New York
Hicksville	The Hicksville Gregory Museum—9,000 specimens from the major mineral groups, also NJ zeolites, Herkimer "diamonds," fluorescents
New York City	American Museum of Natural History—Gems, meteorites, emphasis on exceptional specimens from the U.S.
Pawling	The Gunnison Natural History Museum—Minerals

NORTH CAROLINA

Fee Dig Mines and Guide Services

Almond   Almond   Nantahala Gorge Ruby Mine—Sluice for rubies, sapphires, amethyst, topaz, garnet, citrine, smoky quartz

Boone   Foggy Mountain Gem Mine—Screen for topaz, garnet, aquamarine, peridot, ruby, star sapphire, amethyst, citrine, smoky quartz, tourmaline, emerald

Canton   Old Pressley Sapphire Mine—Sluice for sapphires, zircon, garnet, mica

Cherokee   Smoky Mountain Gold & Ruby Mine—Sluice for gold and gems

Chimney Rock   Chimney Rock Gemstone Mine—Screen for aquamarine, emerald, ruby, peridot, garnet, quartz, agate, hematite, amethyst, sodalite

Franklin   Cowee Mountain Ruby Mine—Sluice for rubies, sapphires, garnets, tourmaline, smoky quartz, amethyst, citrine, moonstone, topaz

Gold City Gem Mine—Sluice for rubies, sapphires, garnets, emeralds, tourmaline, smoky quartz, amethyst, citrine, moonstone, topaz

Mason Mountain Mine and Cowee Gift Shop—Sluice for rhodolite, rubies, sapphires, garnets, kyanite, crystal quartz, smoky quartz, moonstones

Mason's Ruby and Sapphire Mine—Dig and sluice for sapphires (all colors), pink and red rubies

Moon Stone Gem Mine—Sluice for rhodolite garnets, rubies, sapphires, other precious stones

Rocky Face Gem Mine—Sluice for rubies, rhodolite garnets

Rose Creek Mine and Rock Shop—Sluice for rubies, sapphires, garnets, moonstones, amethysts, smoky quartz, citrine, rose quartz, topaz

Sheffield Mine—Sluice for rubies, sapphires, enriched material from around the world

Hiddenite   Emerald Hollow Mine-Hiddenite Gems, Inc.—Sluice for rutile, sapphires, garnets, monazite, hiddenite, smoky quartz, tourmaline, clear quartz, aquamarine, sillimanite

Highlands   Jackson Hole Gem Mine—Sluice for rubies, sapphires, garnets, tourmaline, smoky quartz, amethyst, citrine, moonstone, topaz

**Little
Switzerland**   Blue Ridge Gemstone Mine—Sluice for sapphires, emeralds, rubies, aquamarine, tourmaline, topaz, garnets, amethyst, lepidolite, citrine, moonstone, kyanite, rose, clear, rutilated, and smoky quartz

Emerald Village—Sluice for sapphire, emerald, ruby, aquamarine, tourmaline, topaz, garnet, amethyst, lepidolite, citrine, beryl, moonstone, kyanite, rose, clear, rutilated, and smoky quartz

Marion	Carolina Emerald Mine and Vein Mountain Gold Camp—Mine for gold, emerald, aquamarine, moonstone, feldspar crystals, garnets, smoky, rose, blue, and clear quartz, tourmaline
	Heather Grove Gold and Gem Panning—Pan for gold or a variety of gems and minerals
	The Lucky Strike—Sluice for gems and gold panning
Marshall	Little Pine Garnet Mine—Dig for garnets; can take a horseback ride to the mine
Micaville	Rock Mine Tours—Dig for emeralds, aquamarine, golden beryl, feldspar, pink feldspar, star garnets, biotite, olivine, moonstone, thulite, black tourmaline
Midland	Reed Gold Mine State Historic Site—Gold panning
New London	Cotton Patch Gold Mine—Gold panning
	Mountain Creek Gold Mine—Gold panning
Spruce Pine	Gem Mountain Gemstone Mine—Sluice for sapphires, crabtree emeralds, rubies, Brushy Creek and Wiseman aquamarine
	Rio Doce Gem Mine—Sluice for sapphires, emeralds, rubies, aquamarine, tourmaline, topaz, garnets, amethysts, lepidolite, citrine, beryl, moonstone, kyanite, rose, clear, rutilated, and smoky quartz
	Spruce Pine Gem and Gold Mine—Sluice for sapphires, emeralds, rubies, aquamarine, tourmaline, topaz, garnets, amethyst, lipidolite, citrine, beryl, moonstone, kyanite, rose, clear, rutilated, and smoky quartz
Union Mills	Thermal City Gold Mine—Gold and gemstone panning

Museums and Mine Tours

Asheville	Colburn Earth Science Museum—Collection of mineral specimens from NC and the world
Aurora	Aurora Fossil Museum—Geology of phosphate mine
Franklin	Franklin Gem and Mineral Museum—Specimens from NC and around the world
	Ruby City Gems and Minerals—Specimens from NC and around the world
Gastonia	Schiele Museum—North Carolina gems and minerals
Greensboro	Natural Science Center of Greensboro—Specimens from NC and around the world
Hendersonville	Mineral and Lapidary Museum of Henderson County, Inc.—Minerals and lapidary arts
Linville	Grandfather Mountain Nature Museum—Specimens from NC
Little Switzerland	North Carolina Mining Museum and Mine Tour—Tour a closed feldspar mine

| **Midland** | Reed Gold Mine Historic Site—Gold mine tour |
| **Spruce Pine** | Museum of North Carolina Minerals—Specimens primarily from local mines |

Annual Events

Franklin	Macon County Gemboree—Third weekend in July
	"Leaf Looker" Gemboree—Second weekend in October
Spruce Pine	Original NC Mineral and Gem Festival—Four days at the end of July/beginning of August

NORTH DAKOTA

Fee Dig Mines and Guide Services
> None

Museums and Mine Tours

Beulah	Tours at several area lignite strip mines
Dickinson	Dakota Dinosaur Museum—Displays of rocks and minerals including borax from CA, turquoise from AZ, fluorescent minerals, aurora crystals from AR
Parshall	Paul Broste Rock Museum—Displays of rocks from the area and around the world

OHIO

Fee Dig Mines and Guide Services

| **Hopewell** | Hidden Springs Ranch—Dig for flint (groups only) |
| | Nethers Flint—Dig for flint |

Museums and Mine Tours

Cleveland	The Cleveland Museum of Natural History—The Wade Gallery of Gems and Minerals has over 1,500 gems and minerals
Columbus	Orton Geological Museum—Rocks and minerals from OH and the world
Dayton	Boonshoft Museum of Discovery—Minerals and crystals
Glenford	Flint Ridge State Memorial—Ancient flint quarrying
Lima	Allen County Museum—Rock and mineral exhibit

OKLAHOMA

Fee Dig Mines and Guide Services

| **Kenton** | Black Mesa Bed & Breakfast—Rockhounding on a working cattle ranch |

Howard Layton Ranch—Rockhounding on a working cattle ranch

Museums and Mine Tours

Coalgate   Coal Country Mining and Historical Museum—Mining museum

Enid   The Mr. and Mrs. Dan Midgley Museum—Rock and mineral collection predominantly from OK and the TX shoreline

Noble   Timberlake Rose Rock Museum—Displays of barite roses

Picher   Picher Mining Museum—Lead and zinc mining

Tulsa   Elsing Museum—Gems and minerals

OREGON

Fee Dig Mines and Guide Services

Federal lands   Baker City, Jacksonville, Medford, Salem, Unity—Pan for gold

Klamath Falls   Juniper Ridge Opal Mine—Hunt for fire opal

Madras   Richard's Recreational Ranch—Dig for thundereggs, agate

Mitchell   Lucky Strike Geodes—Dig for thundereggs (picture jasper)

Plush   Dust Devil Mining Co.—Dig for sunstones

Ridge Top Mines—Dig for sunstones

Spectrum Sunstone Mines—Dig for sunstones

Roseburg   Cow Creek Recreational Area—Pan for gold

Yachats   City of Yachats—Beachcombing for agates and jaspers

Museums and Mine Tours

Central Point   Crater Rock Museum—Displays of minerals, thundereggs, fossils, geodes, cut and polished gemstones

Corvallis   Oregon State University Dept. of Geosciences—Mineral displays

Hillsboro   Rice Northwest Museum of Rocks and Minerals—Displays of minerals and crystals

Redmond   Peterson's Rock Garden—Unusual rock specimens, fluorescent display

Sumpter   Sumpter Valley Dredge State Heritage Area—View a gold dredge, tour historic gold mine towns

Annual Events

Cottage Grove   Bohemia Mining Days—Four days in July, gold panning and exposition

Prineville   Rockhounds Pow-Wow—Mid-June

PENNSYLVANIA

Fee Dig Mines and Guide Services

Spring Grove   Jones Geological Services—Guide services for mineral collecting

Museums and Mine Tours

Ashland	Museum of Anthracite Mining—Story of anthracite coal
	Pioneer Tunnel Coal Mine—Tour an anthracite coal mine
Bryn Mawr	Museum, Department of Geology, Bryn Mawr College—Rotating display of 1,500 minerals from a collection of 23,500 specimens
Carlisle	Rennie Geology Museum, Dickinson College—Gem and mineral display
Harrisburg	State Museum of Pennsylvania—Geology of everyday products
Lancaster	North Museum of Natural History and Science—Worldwide specimens with a focus on Lancaster County
Lansford	No. 9 Mine and Museum—Coal mine tour
Media	Delaware County Institute of Science—Minerals from around the world
Patton	Seldom Seen Mine—Tour a bituminous coal mine
Philadelphia	Academy of Natural Science—Exhibit of gems and minerals
	Wagner Free Institute of Science—Rocks and minerals
Pittsburgh	Carnegie Museum of Natural History—One of the premier gem and mineral exhibits in the country
Scranton	Anthracite Museum Complex—Several anthracite coal-related attractions, including mine tours and museums
Tarentum	Tour-Ed Mine—Bituminous coal mine tour
Uniontown	Coal & Coke Heritage Center—Connellsville Coke Region
Waynesburg	Paul R. Stewart Museum, Waynesburg University—Outstanding mineral collection
West Chester	Geology Museum, West Chester University—Specimens from Chester County, fluorescent specimens
Wilkes-Barre	Luzerne County Historical Society—Displays on anthracite coal mining
Windber	Windber Coal Heritage Center—Exhibits present the heritage of coal mining

RHODE ISLAND

Fee Dig Mines and Guide Services
> None

Museums and Mine Tours

Providence	Museum of Natural History and Planetarium—Rocks and minerals

SOUTH CAROLINA

Fee Dig Mines and Guide Services

Antreville	Diamond Hill—Dig your own quartz

Museums and Mine Tours

Charleston   The Charleston Museum—Small display of gems and minerals
Clemson   Bob Campbell Geology Museum—Minerals, meteorites, faceted stones
Columbia   McKissick Museum, University of South Carolina Campus—Exhibits on geology and gemstones
South Carolina State Museum—Small display of rocks and minerals

SOUTH DAKOTA

Fee Dig Mines and Guide Services

Deadwood   Broken Boot Gold Mine—Pan for gold
Hill City   Wade's Gold Mill—Pan for gold
Keystone   Big Thunder Gold Mine—Pan for gold
Lead   Black Hills Mining Museum—Pan for gold
Wall   Buffalo Gap National Grassland—Hunt for agates

Museums and Mine Tours

Deadwood   Broken Boot Gold Mine—Gold mine tour
Hill City   Wade's Gold Mill—Guided tour and displays of mining equipment
Keystone   Big Thunder Gold Mine—Underground mine tour
Lead   Black Hills Mining Museum—Simulated underground mine tour
Homestead Visitors Center—Gold mining displays
Murdo   National Rockhound and Lapidary Hall of Fame—Gems and minerals
Rapid City   Journey Museum—Geology of the Black Hill
South Dakota School of Mines and Technology—Local minerals

TENNESSEE

Fee Dig Mines and Guide Services

Ducktown   Burra Burra Mine—Collect minerals in tailings; garnets, pyite, chalcopyrite, pyrrhotite, actinolite

Museums and Mine Tours

Ducktown   Ducktown Basin Museum—Copper mining heritage
Johnson City   Hands On! Regional Museum—Simulated coal mine
Knoxville   The Frank H. McClung Museum—Geology of Tennessee
Memphis   Memphis Pink Palace Museum—Geology and minerals from famous mid-South localities
Murfreesboro   Middle Tennessee Mineral, Gem, and Fossil Museum—Minerals from Tennessee zinc mines, birthstones, and fluorescent minerals.

TEXAS

Fee Dig Mines and Guide Services

Alpine	Stillwell Ranch—Hunt for agate and jasper
	Woodward Ranch—Hunt for agate, precious opal, and others
Mason	Lindsay Ranch—Hunt for topaz and other minerals
	Seaquist Ranch—Hunt for topaz
Three Rivers	House Ranch—Hunt for agate

Museums and Mine Tours

Alpine	Last Frontier Museum and Antelope Lodge—Display of rocks from West Texas
Austin	Texas Memorial Museum of Science and History—Gems and minerals
Canyon	Panhandle Plains Historical Museum—Gems and minerals from the Texas panhandle
Fort Davis	Chihuahuan Desert Research Institute—Displays on area mining and minerals
Fort Stockton	Annie Riggs Memorial Museum—Rocks and minerals of Pecos County and the Big Bend area
Fritch	Alibates Flint Quarries—View ancient flint quarries
Houston	Houston Museum of Natural Science—Displays of gem and mineral specimens
Marble Falls	Granite Mountain—View marble mining operations
Mckenney	The Heard Natural Science Museum and Wildlife Sanctuary—Rocks and minerals
Odessa	Odessa Meteor Crater—Meteorite crater

UTAH

Fee Dig Mines and Guide Services

Dugway Mountains	Dugway Geode Beds—Dig for geodes
Kanab	Joe's Rock Shop—Dig for septarian nodules

Museums and Mine Tours

Bingham Canyon	Bingham Canyon Mine Visitors Center—Overlook for open-pit copper mine
Eureka	Tintec Mining Museum—Mineral display and mining artifacts
Helper	Western Mining and Railroad Museum—Mining exhibits, simulated 1900 coal mine
Hyrum	Hyrum City Museum—Display of fluorescent minerals

| Lehi | John Hutchings Museum of Natural History—Minerals linked to mining districts, display of uncut gems |
| Salt Lake City | Museum of Natural History—Mineral classification, Utah ores and minerals, fluorescent minerals |

Place of Interest

| Moab | Moab Rock Shop—Information on rockhounding |

VERMONT

Fee Dig Mines and Guide Services

| Ludlow | Camp Plymouth State Park—Gold panning |

Museums and Mine Tours

Barre	Rock of Ages Corporation—Watch granite being quarried
Norwich	Montshire Museum of Science—Fluorescent minerals
Proctor	Vermont Marble Museum—Story of marble

VIRGINIA

Fee Dig Mines and Guide Services

Amelia	Morefield Gem Mine, Inc.—Dig and sluice for garnet, quartz topaz, and many others
Mckenney	Lucky Lake Gem and Mineral Mine of Virginia—Sluice for natural pegmatite minerals and salted material
Stuart	Fairy Stone State Park—Hunt for staurolite crystals (fairy stones)
Virginia City	Virginia City Gem Mine and Museum—Pan for quartz, ruby, sapphire, garnet, gold

Museums and Mine Tours

Big Stone Gap	Harry W. Meador, Jr. Coal Museum—Exhibits and mining equipment
Blacksburg	Virginia Tech Geosciences Museum—Large display of Virginia minerals
Goldvein	Monroe Park—Tour a mine camp, gold panning demonstrations
Harrisonburg	The James Madison University Mineral Museum—Crystals, gems, fluorescent display, specimens from Amelia
Martinsville	Stone Cross Mountain Museum—A museum of "Fairy Crosses," specimens of staurolite
	Virginia Museum of Natural History—Minerals and mining exhibits
Pocahontas	Pocahontas Exhibition Coal Mine and Museum—Coal mine tour
Richmond	University of Richmond Museums—Displays Virginia minerals and a 2,400-carat blue topaz

WASHINGTON

Fee Dig Mines and Guide Services
Olympia   Baker-Snoqualmie National Forest—Pan for gold
Ravensdale   Geology Adventures, Inc.—Field trips; collect quartz, garnets, topaz, and others

Museums and Mine Tours
Castle Rock Mount St. Helens National Volcanic Monument—Focus on geology
Ellensburg   Kittitas County Historical Museum and Society—Polished rocks
Pullman   Washington State University—Silicified wood, minerals
Seattle   Burke Museum of Natural History and Culture—Rocks, minerals, the geology of Washington, and a walk-through volcano

WEST VIRGINIA

Fee Dig Mines and Guide Services
None

Museums and Mine Tours
Beckley   The Beckley Exhibition Coal Mine—Tour a bituminous coal mine
Charleston   The Avampato Discovery Museum at the Clay Center—Exhibits show the story behind West Virginia's geology
Morgantown   Museum of Geology and Natural History; W. V. Geological and Economic Survey—Geology of West Virginia

WISCONSIN

Fee Dig Mines and Guide Services
None

Museums and Mine Tours
Dodgeville   The Museum of Minerals and Crystals—Local mineral specimens, specimens from around the world
Hurley   Iron County Historical Museum—History of area mining, last remaining mine head frame in Wisconsin
Madison   Geology Museum, University of Wisconsin at Madison—Minerals, fluorescent minerals, model of Wisconsin cave
Menasha   Weis Earth Science Museum, University of Wisconsin, Fox Valley—Official state mineralogical museum of Wisconsin
Milwaukee   Milwaukee Public Museum—Displays of geological specimens

	University of Wisconsin at Milwaukee—Minerals
Plateville	The Mining Museum—Lead and zinc mining in the upper Mississippi Valley
Potosi	St. John Mine (Wisconsin's 1825 Lead Rush)—Lead mine guided tour
Stevens Point	Museum of Natural History, University of Wisconsin—Stevens Point rock and mineral display

Annual Events

Neenah	Quarry Quest—Kid-oriented collecting activities, held in September and sponsored by the Weis Museum, the University of Wisconsin, Fox Valley
Menasha	Wonderful World of Agates Symposium—International symposium on Agates, held in July, sponsored by the Weis Musuem, the University of Wisconsin, Fox Valley

WYOMING

Fee Dig Mines and Guide Services

Shell	Trapper Galloway Ranch—Dig for moss agate

Museums and Mine Tours

Casper	Tate Geological Museum—Rocks and minerals, including Wyoming jade, and fluorescent minerals
Cheyenne	Wyoming State Museum—Minerals of Wyoming, coal "swamp"
Laramie	Geological Museum, University of Wyoming—Rocks and minerals, fluorescent minerals from Wyoming
Saratoga	Saratoga Museum—Minerals from around the world, local geology
Worland	Washaki Museum—Geology of Big Horn Basin

Annual Events

Casper	Tate Geological Museum Symposium on Wyoming Geology—June

Index by Gems and Minerals

This index lists all the gems and minerals that can be found at fee dig mines in the U.S., and shows the city and state where the mine is located. To use the index, look up the gem or mineral you are interested in, and note the states and cities where they are located. Then go to the state and city to find the name of the mine, and information about the mine.

The following notes provide additional information:

(#)   A number in parentheses is the number of mines in that town that have that gem or mineral.

(*)   Gem or mineral is found in the state, but the mine may also add material to the ore. Check with the individual mine for confirmation.

(FT)   Field trip.

(GS)   Guide service (location listed is the location of the guide service, not necessarily the location of the gems or minerals being collected).

(I)   Mineral has been identified at the mine site but may be difficult to find.

(M)   Museum that allows collection of one specimen as a souvenir.

(MM)   Micromount (a very small crystal which, when viewed under a microscope or magnifying glass, is found to be a high-quality crystal).

(O)   Available at mine but comes from other mines.

(R)   Can be found, but is rare.

(S)   Not the main gem or mineral for which the site is known.

(SA)   "Salted" or enriched gem or mineral.

(U)   Unique to the site.

(Y)   Yearly collecting event.

Actinolite Tennessee: Ducktown

Agate Arkansas: Murfreesboro (S); Michigan: Grand Marais; Montana: Helena (S); New Mexico: Deming; North Carolina: Chimney Rock; Oklahoma: Kenton (2); Oregon: Madras, Yachats; South Dakota: Wall; Texas: Three Rivers
Banded agate Texas: Alpine; New Mexico: Gila

Fire agate Arizona: Safford (2)
Iris agate Texas: Alpine
Ledge agate Oregon: Madras
Moss agate Oregon: Madras, Mitchell; Texas: Alpine (2); Wyoming: Shell
Polka-dot Jasp-agate Oregon: Madras
Plume agate Nevada: Reno (GS)
Pompom agate Texas: Alpine
Rainbow agate Oregon: Madras
Red plume agate Texas: Alpine

Albite Maine: Bethel, Poland (GS), West Paris; New Hampshire: Grafton (I); New Mexico: Dixon

Albite (Cleavelandite Var.) Maine: Poland (GS)

Amazonite Virginia: Amelia

Amber Texas: Mason (R); Washington: Ravensdale (GS)

Amethyst Arizona: Glendale; Arkansas: Mt. Ida (SA), Murfreesboro (S); Georgia: Cleveland; Maine: Bethel (R), West Paris; Montana: Dillon; Nevada: Reno (GS); New Hampshire: Grafton (I), Laconia; North Carolina (*): Almond, Boone, Cherokee, Chimney Rock, Franklin (3), Highlands, Little Switzerland, Spruce Pine (3); South Carolina: Antreville

Amethyst scepters Arizona: Tempe

Amblygonite Maine: West Paris

Amphibolite New Hampshire: Grafton (I)

Andesite New Mexico: Gila

Apatite Maine: Auburn, Bethel, Poland (GS), West Paris; New Hampshire: Grafton; New Mexico: Dixon
  Fluorapatite Maine: Poland (GS)
  Hydroxylapatite Maine: Poland (GS)
  Purple apatite Maine: West Paris

Aplite New Hampshire: Grafton (I)

Aquamarine California: Pala; Georgia: LaGrange; Maine: Bethel, Poland (GS); New Hampshire: Grafton (I); North Carolina (*): Boone, Chimney Rock, Franklin, Hiddenite, Little Switzerland (2), Marion, Micaville, Spruce Pine (2) (FT)
  Brushy Creek Aquamarine North Carolina: Spruce Pine (I) (FT)
  Weisman aquamarine North Carolina: Spruce Pine (I) (FT)

Aragonite Arizona: Glendale (GS)

Arsenopyrite Maine: Poland (GS)

Augelite Maine: Poland (GS)

Aurichalcite New Mexico: Magdalena

Autenite Maine: Auburn, Bethel, Poland (GS); New Hampshire: Grafton (I)

Azurite New Mexico: Magdalena

Barite Arizona: Glendale (GS); Arkansas: Murfreesboro (S); Georgia: Lincolnton; New Mexico: Bingham; Washington: Ravensdale (GS)

Benitoite California: Coalinga

Beraumite Maine: Poland (GS)

Bermanite Maine: Poland (GS)

Bertrandite Maine: Poland (GS), West Paris

Bertranite New Hampshire: Grafton (I)

Beryl Delaware: Wilmngton; Georgia: LaGrange; Maine: Auburn, Bethel, Poland (GS), West Paris; New Hampshire: Grafton (I); New Mexico: Dixon; North Carolina (*): Little Switzerland (2), Spruce Pine (2); Virginia: Amelia
  Aqua beryl New Hampshire: Grafton (I)
  Blue beryl (see also aquamarine) New Hampshire: Grafton (I)
  Golden beryl North Carolina: Spruce Pine (FT); New Hampshire: Grafton (I)

Beryllonite Maine: Poland (GS), West Paris

Beta-Uranophane New Hampshire: Grafton

Biotite Maine: Bethel; New Hampshire: Grafton (I); North Carolina: Micaville

Borate California: Boron (Y)

Bornite New Hampshire: Grafton (I)

Brazillianite Maine: Poland (GS)

Brochantite New Mexico: Bingham

Cacoxenite Georgia: Lincolnton

Calcite Arizona: Glendale (GS); Arkansas: Murfreesboro (S); Florida: Ft. Drum; Michigan: Ontonagon; New Hampshire: Grafton; New Mexico: Bingham; New York: Middleville; Texas: Mason; Virginia: Amelia

Cape May "diamonds" See Quartz

Casserite Maine: Poland (GS)

Cassiterite Maine: West Paris; Texas: Mason

Chalcedony Arizona: Safford; Nevada: Reno (GS); New Mexico: Deming
  White New Mexico: Gila
  Pink New Mexico: Gila
  Chalcedony roses New Mexico: Gila

Chalcopyrite Tennessee: Ducktown

Childrenite Maine: Poland (GS)

Chrysoberyl New Hampshire: Grafton (I)

Chrysocolla Arizona: Glendale (GS)

Citrine North Carolina (*): Almond, Boone, Cherokee, Franklin (3), Highlands, Little Switzerland, Spruce Pine (3); Virginia: McKenney

Clarkite New Hampshire: Grafton (I)

Clevelandite California: Pala; Maine: Auburn, Poland (GS), West Paris; New Hampshire: Grafton (I); New Mexico: Dixon

Columbite New Hampshire: Grafton (I); Maine: Bethel, Poland (GS), West Paris

Compotite New Hampshire: Grafton (I)

Cookeite Maine: West Paris

Copper, pure Michigan: Ontonagon, Mohawk

Copper minerals Michigan: Mohawk (M); New Mexico: Magdalena

Crandalite Georgia: Lincolnton

Cryolite New Hampshire: Grafton (I)

Cymatolite New Hampshire: Grafton (I)

Datolite Michigan: Ontonagon

Dendrites New Hampshire: Grafton (I)

Diadochite Maine: Poland (GS)

Diamond Arkansas: Murfreesboro

Dickinsonite Maine: Poland (GS)

Djurleite California: Coalinga

Dolomite crystals New York: Middleville

Earlshannonite Maine: Poland (GS)

Elabite See listing under Tourmaline

Emerald Arkansas: Mt. Ida (SA); Georgia: Cleveland (SA), Dahlonega (SA); North Carolina (*): Almond, Boone, Cherokee, Chimney Rock, Franklin (2), Highlands, Little Switzerland (2), Marion, Micaville, Spruce Pine (2)

    Crabtree emerald North Carolina: Spruce Pine

Eosphorite Maine: Poland (GS)

Epidote Michigan: Ontonagon; Texas: Mason

Fairfieldite Maine: Poland (GS)

Fairy stones (See Staurolite crystals)

Feldspar Delaware: Wilmington; New Hampshire: Grafton (I); North Carolina: Marion, Micaville; Virginia: Amelia

    Albite feldspar Maine: Bethel

Flint Ohio: Hopewell (2)

Fluoroapatite New Hampshire: Grafton (I)

Fluorescent minerals Arizona: Glendale (GS); Kentucky: Marian; New Jersey: Franklin, Ogdensburg; North Carolina: Little Switzerland; Washington: Ravensdale (GS)

Fluorite Arizona: Glendale (GS); Illinois: Rosiclare; Kentucky: Marion; New Mexico: Bingham; Virginia: Amelia; Washington: Ravensdale (GS)

Franklinite New Jersey: Franklin

Fuchsite Georgia: Lincolnton

Gahnite (spinel) Maine: Poland (GS), West Paris

Gainsite Maine: Poland (GS)

Galena Arizona: Glendale (GS); New Mexico: Bingham; Texas: Mason

Garnets Alaska: Juneau; Arizona: Tempe; California: Pala; Connecticut: Roxbury; Delaware: Wilmington; Georgia: Dahlonega (SA); Idaho: St. Maries; Maine: Auburn, Bethel, Poland (GS), West Paris; Montana: Alder, Helena (S); Nevada: Ely; New Hampshire: Grafton (I); New Mexico: Dixon; New York: North River; North Carolina (*): Almond, Boone, Canton, Cherokee, Chimney Rock, Franklin (4), Marshal, Hiddenite, Highlands, Little Switzerland (2), Marion, Spruce Pine (3) (FT); Tennessee: Ducktown; Texas: Mason; Virginia: McKenney, Virginia City (SA); Washington: Ravensdale (GS)
Almandine garnets Maine: Bethel, Poland (GS); Nevada: Ely
Pyrope garnets North Carolina: Franklin
Rhodolite garnets North Carolina: Franklin

Garnets, Star Idaho: Moscow (GS), St. Maries

Geodes Arizona: Safford; Illinois: Hamilton; Missouri: Alexandria; New Mexico: Deming, Gila; Utah: Dugway Mountains
Lined with:
Agate, blue New Mexico: Deming
Aragonite Illinois: Hamilton; Missouri: Alexandria
Barite Illinois:Hamilton; Missouri: Alexandria
Calcite Missouri: Alexandria
Chalcedony New Mexico: Deming
Dolomite Missouri: Alexandria
Goethite Missouri: Alexandria
Hematite Missouri: Alexandria
Kaoline Missouri: Alexandria
Kaolinite Illinois: Hamilton
Opal, common New Mexico: Deming
Pyrite Missouri: Alexandria
Quartz Illinois: Hamilton; New Mexico: Deming
Selenite needles Missouri: Alexandria
Sphalerite Missouri: Alexandria

Gold (*) Alabama: Cragford; Alaska: Anchorage, Chugach, Chicken, Copper Center, Fairbanks (3), Girdwood, Juneau, McGrath, Nome, Skagway (2), Talkeetna; Arizona: Apache Junction, Goldfield, Prescott, Wickenburg; California: Coloma, Columbia, Jackson, Jamestown, Mariposa, Nevada City, Pine Grove, Placerville; Colorado: Breckenridge, Granite, Idaho Springs (2), Ouray, Silverton; Georgia: Cleveland, Dahlonega (2), Gainesville; Indiana: Knightstown; Montana: Libby,

Philipsburg; New Mexico: Gila; North Carolina: Cherokee, Marion (3), Midland, New London (2), Union Mills; Oregon: Baker City, Halfway, Jacksonville, Medford, Roseburg, Salem, Unity; South Dakota: Deadwood, Hill City, Keystone, Lead; Virginia: Virginia City (SA); Vermont: Plymouth

Gold ore Colorado: Lakewood (M)

Gossanite (clear beryl) California: Pala

Goyazite Maine: Poland (GS)

Graftonite Maine: Poland (GS); New Hampshire: Grafton (I)

Granite, graphic Maine: Auburn

Gummite New Hampshire: Grafton (I)

Hedenburgite New Mexico: Magdalena

Hematite Georgia: Lincolnton; Montana: Helena; New Mexico: Magdalena; North Carolina: Chimney Rock (SA)
    Massive New Mexico: Gila
    Hematite (banded welded tuft) New Mexico: Gila

Herderite, hydroxyl Maine: Bethel, Poland (GS), West Paris

Herkimer "diamonds" See Quartz

Heterosite Maine: Poland (GS)

Hiddenite (spodumene) California: Pala; North Carolina: Hiddenite

Hureaylite Maine: Poland (GS)

Ilmenite Georgia: Lincolnton

Iron minerals New Mexico: Magdalena

Iron ore Michigan: Iron Mountain (M)

Jade California: Pine Grove

Jadite Montana: Helana (S)

Jahnsite Maine: Poland (GS)

Jasper Arkansas: Murfreesboro (S); California: Pine Grove; Montana: Helena (S); Oklahoma: Kenton; Oregon: Madras, Yachats; Texas: Alpine
    Brown Jasper New Mexico: Deming, Gila
    Chocolate jasper New Mexico: Deming
    Jasper breccia New Mexico: Gila
    Orange jasper New Mexico: Deming
    Picture jasper Oregon: Mitchell
    Pink jasper New Mexico: Deming
    Red jasper New Mexico: Gila
    Variegated jasper New Mexico: Deming
    Yellow jasper New Mexico: Deming, Gila

Joaquinite California: Coalinga

Kasolite New Hampshire: Grafton (I)

Kosnarite Maine: Poland (GS)

Kunzite California: Pala

Kyanite Georgia: Lincolnton; North Carolina (*): Franklin, Little Switzerland

Laboradorite Texas: Alpine

Lake County "diamonds" See Quartz

Landsite Maine: Poland (GS)

Laueite Maine: Poland (GS)

Lazulite Georgia: Lincolnton

Lepidolite Maine: Poland (GS), West Paris; New Mexico: Dixon; North Carolina (*): Little Switzerland
   Lemon yellow lepidolite New Hampshire: Grafton (I)
   Purple lepidolite California: Pala

Lepidomelane New Hampshire: Grafton (I)

Limonite Arizona: Tempe; New Mexico: Gila

Linarite New Mexico: Bingham

Lithiophyllite Maine: Poland (GS); New Hampshire: Grafton (I)

Lollingite Maine: Poland (GS)

Ludlamite Maine: Poland (GS)

Magnesium oxide See Psilomellane

Malachite New Mexico: Magdalena

Manganapatite New Hampshire: Grafton (I)

Manganese minerals New Mexico: Deming

Manganese oxide minerals New Mexico: Deming

Marcasite New Hampshire: Grafton (I)

McCrillsite Maine: Poland (GS)

Mica Delaware: Wilmington; California: Pala; Maine: Auburn, Bethel, Poland (GS); New Hampshire: Grafton (I), Laconia; North Carolina: Canton; Virginia: Amelia
   Biotite mica Maine: Bethel, Poland (GS)
   Book mica California: Pala
   Muscovite mica California: Pala; Maine: Poland (GS)

Microcline Maine: Poland (GS)

Microlite New Mexico: Dixon

Mitridatite Maine: Poland (GS)

Molybdenite New Hampshire: Grafton (I)

Montebrasite Maine: Poland (GS)

Montmorillonite Maine: Poland (GS), West Paris; New Hampshire: Grafton (I)

Monzaite Maine: Poland (GS)

Moonstone North Carolina (*): Franklin (4), Highlands, Little Switzerland, Marion, Micaville, Spruce Pine

Moraesite Maine: Poland (GS)

Morganite California: Pala; Maine: Poland (GS)

Muscovite California: Pala; Georgia: Lincolnton; New Hampshire: Grafton (I); New Mexico: Dixon

Natrolite California: Coalinga

Neptunite California: Coalinga

Olivine North Carolina: Micaville

Opal
    Black fire opal Nevada: Denio
    Common opal New Mexico: Deming
    Crystal opal Nevada: Denio
    Fire opal Nevada: Denio (4), Reno (GS); Oregon: Klamath Falls
    Hyalite opal Maine: Bethel
    Precious opal Idaho: Spencer; Texas: Alpine
    Virgin Valley opal Nevada: Reno (GS)
    White opal Nevada: Denio
    Wood opal Nevada: Denio

Perhamite Maine: Poland (GS)

Parsonite New Hampshire: Grafton (I)

Perlite (black to gray) New Mexico: Deming

Peridot Arkansas: Murfreesboro (S); North Carolina (*): Boone, Chimney Rock, Franklin

Petalite Maine: Poland (GS), West Paris

Phenakite Virginia: Amelia

Phosphosiderite Georgia: Lincolnton; Maine: Poland (GS)

Phosphouranylite Maine: Poland (GS)

Phosphyanylite New Hampshire: Grafton (I)

Pitch Stone (with seams of red and brown) New Mexico: Deming

Pollucite Maine: Poland (GS), West Paris

Psilomelane New Hampshire: Grafton (I)

Purpurite Maine: Poland (GS); New Hampshire: Grafton (I)

Pyrite Georgia: Lincolnton; Maine: Bethel, Poland (GS); New Hampshire: Grafton (I); New Mexico: Magdalena; Tennessee: Ducktown; Virginia: Amelia; Washington: Ravensdale (GS)

Pyrophyllite Georgia: Lincolnton

Pyrrhotite New Hampshire: Grafton (I); Tennessee: Ducktown

Quartz Arizona: Glendale (GS), Tempe; Arkansas: Jessieville (3), Mt. Ida (6) (Y), Murfreesboro (S), Pencil Bluff, Story (2); California: Pine Grove; Delaware: Wilmington; Georgia: Lincolnton; Maine: Auburn, Poland (GS), West Paris; Michigan: Ontonagon; Montana: Dillon, Helena (S); New Hampshire: Laconia; New Mexico: Bingham, Deming, Dixon; North Carolina: Franklin; Texas: Alpine, Mason; Virginia: Amelia, Virginia City (SA); Washington: Ravensdale (GS)

  Blue Georgia: Lincolnton; North Carolina: Marion
  Clear Georgia: LaGrange; North Carolina (*): Hiddenite, Little Switzerland, Marion, Spruce Pine
  Milky Maine: Bethel
  Parallel growth Maine: West Paris
  Pseudocubic crystals Maine: West Paris
  Rose Maine: Bethel; New Hampshire: Grafton (I); North Carolina (*): Franklin
  Rutilated North Carolina (*): Little Switzerland, Spruce Pine
  Skeletal quartz South Carolina: Antreville
  Smoky Maine: Bethel; Nevada: Reno (GS); New Hampshire: Grafton, Laconia; North Carolina (*): Almond, Boone, Cherokee, Chimney Rock, Franklin (4), Hiddenite, Highlands, Little Switzerland (2), Marion, Spruce Pine (2); Virginia: McKenney
  Smoky (gem quality) New Hampshire: Grafton (I); South Carolina: Antreville

Quartz "diamonds"

  Lake Co. "diamonds" (moon tears) California: Lake County
  Cape May "diamonds" New Jersey: Cape May
  Herkimer "diamonds" New York: Herkimer, Middleville, St. Johnsville

Reddingite Maine: Poland (GS)

Rhodochrosite Maine: Poland (GS)

Rhodolite (garnet) North Carolina: Franklin

Rhyolite, banded New Mexico: Gila

Rochbridgeite Maine: Poland (GS)

Rose rocks See Barite

Rubies Arkansas: Mt. Ida (SA); California: Pine Grove; Georgia: Cleveland, Dahlonega (SA); Montana: Helena; North Carolina (*):Almond, Boone, Cherokee, Chimney Rock, Franklin (8), Highlands, Little Switzerland (2), Spruce Pine (3);Virginia: Virginia City (SA)

Rutile Georgia: Lincolnton; Maine: Bethel, Poland (GS); North Carolina: Hiddenite

Safflorite New Hampshire: Grafton (I)

Sapphires Georgia: Cleveland (SA), Dahlonega (SA); Montana: Clinton (GS), Hamilton, Helena, Philipsburg (3); North Carolina (*): Almond, Cherokee, Franklin (8), Hiddenite, Highlands, Little Switzerland (2), Spruce Pine (2); Virginia: Virginia City (SA)

  Sapphire, blue North Carolina: Canton

Sapphire, grey North Carolina: Canton
Sapphire, white North Carolina: Canton
Sapphire, bronze North Carolina: Canton
Sapphire, pink North Carolina: Canton
Star sapphire North Carolina: Boone (SA)

Scheelite Maine: West Paris

Scoria New Mexico: Gila

Selenite crystals New Mexico: Bingham

Septarian nodules Utah: Kanab

Serpentine Montana: Helena (S)

Siderite Maine: Bethel

Silica minerals New Mexico: Deming

Sillimanite New Hampshire: Grafton (I); North Carolina (*): Hiddenite

Silver Michigan: Ontonagon

Smithsonite Arizona: Glendale (GS)

Sodalite North Carolina: Chimney Rock (SA)

Soddylite New Hampshire: Grafton (I)

Spangolite New Mexico: Bingham

Spessartine New Mexico: Dixon

Spinel Montana: Alder

Spodumene Maine: Poland (GS), West Paris; New Mexico: Dixon
   Altered spodumene Maine: West Paris
   Hiddenite California: Pala; North Carolina: Hiddenite

Staurolite New Hampshire: Grafton (I); Virginia: Stuart

Stewartite Maine: Poland (GS)

Strengite Georgia: Lincolnton

Strunzite Maine: Poland (GS)

Sulfur Georgia: Lincolnton

Sunstone Nevada: Reno (GS); Oregon: Plush (3)

Switzerite Maine: Poland (GS)

Tantalite-Columbite Virginia: Amelia

Thulite North Carolina: Micaville

Thundereggs New Mexico: Deming; Oregon: Madras, Mitchell

Tobernite New Hampshire: Grafton (I)

Topaz Georgia: Cleveland (SA); Maine: Poland (GS); Montana: Helena; New Hampshire: Grafton (I); North Carolina (*): Almond, Boone, Cherokee, Franklin (2), Little

Switzerland, Marion, Spruce Pine (3); Texas: Mason (2); Virginia: Amelia, McKenney
Pink topaz Washington: Ravensdale (GS)

Torberite Maine: Poland (GS)

Tourmaline Arizona: Tempe; California: Mesa Grande; Maine: Auburn (2), Poland (GS), West Paris; New Hampshire: Grafton (I); North Carolina (*): Boone, Franklin (2), Little Switzerland, Marion, Spruce Pine (3); Texas: Mason; Virginia: Amelia, McKenney
Bi-colored California: Pala
Black tourmaline California: Pala; Georgia: LaGrange; Maine: Auburn, Bethel, Poland (GS), West Paris; New Hampshire: Grafton (I); North Carolina: Spruce Pine (FT)
Gem tourmaline Maine: West Paris
Green tourmaline California: Pala; Maine: West Paris
Pink tourmaline California: Pala

Triphyllite Maine: Poland (GS), West Paris; New Hampshire: Grafton (I)

Triplite Maine: Poland (GS)

Turquoise Nevada: Reno (GS)

Uralolite Maine: Poland (GS)

Uranite Maine: Bethel, Poland (GS); New Hampshire: Grafton (I) (species with gummite-world-famous)

Uranium minerals New Hampshire: Grafton (I); North Carolina: Little Switzerland

Uranophane New Hampshire: Grafton (I)

Vandendriesscheite New Hampshire: Grafton (I)

Variscite Georgia: Lincolnton; Nevada: Reno (GS)

Vesuvianite Maine: West Paris (I)

Vivianite New Hampshire: Grafton (I); Maine: Poland (GS)

Voelerkenite New Hampshire: Grafton (I)

Volcanic Bombs New Mexico: Gila

Wardilite Maine: Poland (GS)

Whitlockite Maine: Poland (GS)

Whitmoreite Maine: Poland (GS)

Willemite Arizona: Glendale (GS)

Woodhouseite Georgia: Lincolnton

Wodginite Maine: Poland (GS)

Wulfenite Arizona: Glendale (GS)

Zeolites New Mexico: Gila

Zircon Maine: Bethel, Poland (GS), West Paris; New Hampshire: Grafton (I); North Carolina: Canton; Texas: Mason

Annual Events

JANUARY

Quartzite, AZ, Gem and Mineral Shows—January–February

Tucson, AZ, Gem and Mineral Shows—End of January–mid-February

FEBRUARY

Quartzsite, AZ, Gem and Mineral Shows—January–February

Tucson, AZ, Gem and Mineral Shows—End of January–mid-February

MARCH

Boron, CA, Rock Bonanza—Weekend before Easter

Scottsdale, AZ, Minerals of Arizona—Symposium 1 day in March or April

APRIL

Boron, CA, Rock Bonanza—Weekend before Easter

Dahlonega, GA, World Open Gold Panning Championship—Third Saturday of April

Scottsdale, AZ, Minerals of Arizona—Symposium 1 day in March or April

MAY

Augusta, ME, Maine Mineral Symposium—Second full weekend in May

Poland, ME, Maine Pegmatite Workshop—One week at the end of May or beginning of June

JUNE

Casper, WY, Tate Geological Museum Symposium on Wyoming Geology

Poland, ME, Maine Pegmatite Workshop—One week at the end of May or beginning of June

Prineville, OR, Rockhounds Pow-Wow—Mid-June

JULY

Cottage Grove, OR, Bohemia Mining Days—Four days in July

Franklin, NC, Macon County Gemboree—Third weekend in July

Menasha, WI, Wonderful World of Agate Symposium—July

Moose Lake, MN, Agate Days—One weekend in July

AUGUST

Houghton, MI, Copper County Mineral Retreat—One week in early August

Spruce Pine, NC, Original North Carolina Mineral and Gem Festival—Four days at the beginning of August

SEPTEMBER

Coloma, CA, Marshall Gold Discovery State Historic Park: Gold Rush Live—End of September–beginning of October

Neenah, WI, Quarry Quest—September

OCTOBER

Coloma, CA, Marshall Gold Discovery State Historic Park: Gold Rush Live—End of September–beginning of October

Dahlonega, GA, Gold Rush Days—Third weekend in October

Franklin, NC, "Leaf Looker" Gemboree—Second weekend in October

Jasper, GA, Pickens County Marble Festival—First weekend in October

Keokuk, IA, Rocktober Geode Fest—One weekend in early October

Mt. Ida, AR, Quartz Crystal Festival and World Championship Dig—Second weekend in October

NOVEMBER

Socorro, NM, New Mexico Mineral Symposium—Two days in November

DECEMBER

No information available.

State Gem and Mineral Symbols

STATE	GEMSTONE	MINERAL	STONE/ROCK
Alabama	Star Blue Quartz (1990)	Hematite (1967)	Marble (1969)
Alaska	Jade (1968)	Gold (1968)	
Arizona	Turquoise (1974)	Fire agate	Petrified Wood
Arkansas	Diamond	Quartz crystal	Bauxite
California	Benitoite	Gold	Serpentine (1965)
Colorado	Aquamarine (1971)	Rhodochrosite	Yule Marble
Connecticut	Garnet (1977)		
Delaware			Sillimanite
Florida	Moonstone		Agatized coral
Georgia	Amethyst	Staurolite	Quartz
Hawaii	Black Coral		Lava
Idaho	Star Garnet (1967)		
Illinois		Fluorite (1965)	
Indiana			Limestone
Iowa			Geode
Kansas			
Kentucky	Freshwater Pearl	Coal	Kentucky Agate
Louisiana	Agate		Petrified Palm
Maine	Tourmaline (1971)		
Maryland		Patuxent River Stone	
Massachusetts	Rhodonite	Babingtonite	Plymouth Rock, Dighton Rock, Roxbury Conglomerate
Michigan	Isle Royal Greenstone (Chlorostrolite) (1972)		Petosky Stone (1965)
Minnesota	Lake Superior Agate	Iron	
Mississippi			Petrified Wood (1976)
Missouri		Galena (1967)	Mozarkite (1967)

STATE	GEMSTONE	MINERAL	STONE/ROCK
Montana	Yogo Sapphire & Agate (1969)		
Nebraska	Blue Agate (1967)		Prairie Agate (1967)
Nevada	Virgin Valley Blackfire Opal (1987) (Precious) Turquoise (1987) (Semiprecious)	Silver (Official Metal)	Sandstone (1987)
New Hampshire	Smoky Quartz	Beryl	Granite
New Jersey			Stockton Sandstone
New Mexico	Turquoise (1967)		
New York	Garnet (1969)		
North Carolina	Emerald (1973)		Granite/Unakite
North Dakota			Teredo Wood
Ohio	Flint (1965)		
Oklahoma			Barite Rose
Oregon	Sunstone (1987)		Thundereggs (1965)
Pennsylvania			
Rhode Island		Bowenite	Cumberlandite
South Carolina	Amethyst		Blue Granite
South Dakota	Fairburn Agate (1966)	Rose Quartz (1966) (Mineral/Stone)	
Tennessee	Tennessee River Pearls		Tennessee Limestone and Agate
Texas	Texas Blue Topaz (1969) Lone Star Cut (1977) (Gemstone Cut)		Petrified Palmwood (1960)
Utah	Topaz	Copper	Coal
Vermont	Grossular Garnet	Talc	Granite, Marble, Slate
Virginia			
Washington	Petrified Wood (1975)		
West Virginia	Mississippian Coral, Lithostrotionella		
Wisconsin		Galena (1971)	Wausau Red Granite (1971)
Wyoming	Nephrite Jade (1967)		

Finding Your Own Birthstone

Following is a listing of fee dig sites presented in this four-volume guide where you can find your birthstone! Refer to the individual mine listings for more information on individual mines.

Garnet (January Birthstone) Alaska: Juneau; Arizona: Tempe; California: Pala; Connecticut: Roxbury; Delaware: Wilmington; Georgia: Dahlonega (SA); Idaho: St. Maries; Maine: Auburn, Bethel, Poland (GS), West Paris; Montana: Alder, Helena (S); Nevada: Ely; New Hampshire: Grafton (I); New Mexico: Dixon; New York: North River; North Carolina (*): Almond, Boone, Canton, Cherokee, Chimney Rock, Franklin (4), Marshal, Hiddenite, Highlands, Little Switzerland (2), Marion, Spruce Pine (3) (FT); Tennessee: Ducktown; Texas: Mason; Virginia: McKenney, Virginia City (SA); Washington: Ravensdale (GS)
  Almandine garnets Maine: Bethel, Poland (GS); Nevada: Ely
  Pyrope garnets North Carolina: Franklin
  Rhodolite garnets North Carolina: Franklin

Garnets, star Idaho: Moscow (GS), St. Maries

Amethyst (February Birthstone) Arizona: Glendale; Arkansas: Mt. Ida (SA), Murfreesboro (S); Georgia: Cleveland; Maine: Bethel (R), West Paris; Montana: Dillon; Nevada: Reno (GS); New Hampshire: Grafton (I), Laconia; North Carolina (*): Almond, Boone, Cherokee, Chimney Rock, Franklin (3), Highlands, Little Switzerland, Spruce Pine (3); South Carolina: Antreville

Amethyst scepters Arizona: Tempe

Aquamarine or Bloodstone (March Birthstone)

Aquamarine California: Pala; Georgia: LaGrange; Maine: Bethel, Poland (GS); New Hampshire: Grafton (I); North Carolina (*):Boone, Chimney Rock, Franklin, Hiddenite, Little Switzerland (2), Marion, Micaville, Spruce Pine (2) (FT)
  Brushy Creek aquamarine North Carolina: Spruce Pine (I) (FT)
  Weisman aquamarine North Carolina: Spruce Pine (I) (FT)

Bloodstone No listing

Diamond (April Birthstone) Arkansas: Murfreesboro

Emerald (May Birthstone) Arkansas: Mt. Ida (SA); Georgia: Cleveland (SA), Dahlonega (SA); North Carolina (*): Almond, Boone, Cherokee, Chimney Rock, Franklin (2), Highlands, Little Switzerland (2), Marion, Micaville, Spruce Pine (2)
  Crabtree emerald North Carolina: Spruce Pine

Moonstone or Pearl (June Birthstone)

Moonstone North Carolina (*): Franklin (4), Highlands, Little Switzerland, Marion, Micaville, Spruce Pine

Pearl No listing

Ruby (July Birthstone) Arkansas: Mt. Ida (SA); California: Pine Grove; Georgia: Cleveland, Dahlonega (SA); Montana: Helena; North Carolina (*): Almond, Boone, Cherokee, Chimney Rock, Franklin (8), Highlands, Little Switzerland (2), Spruce Pine (3);Virginia: Virginia City (SA)

Peridot or Sardonyx (August Birthstone)

Peridot Arkansas: Murfreesboro (S); North Carolina (*): Boone, Chimney Rock, Franklin

Sardonyx No listing

Sapphire (September Birthstone) Georgia: Cleveland (SA), Dahlonega (SA); Montana: Clinton (GS), Hamilton, Helena, Philipsburg (3); North Carolina (*): Almond, Cherokee, Franklin (8), Hiddenite, Highlands, Little Switzerland (2), Spruce Pine (2); Virginia: Virginia City (SA)
    Sapphire, blue North Carolina: Canton
    Sapphire, grey North Carolina: Canton
    Sapphire, white North Carolina: Canton
    Sapphire, bronze North Carolina: Canton
    Sapphire, pink North Carolina: Canton
    Star sapphire North Carolina: Boone (SA)

Opal or Tourmaline (October Birthstone)
Opal
    Black fire opal Nevada: Denio
    Common opal New Mexico: Deming
    Crystal opal Nevada: Denio
    Fire opal Nevada: Denio (4), Reno (GS); Oregon: Klamath Falls
    Hyalite opal Maine: Bethel
    Precious opal Idaho: Spencer; Texas: Alpine
    Virgin Valley opal Nevada: Reno (GS)
    White opal Nevada: Denio
    Wood opal Nevada: Denio
Tourmaline Arizona: Tempe; California: Mesa Grande; Maine: Auburn (2), Poland (GS), West Paris; New Hampshire: Grafton (I); North Carolina (*): Boone, Franklin (2), Little Switzerland, Marion, Spruce Pine (3); Texas: Mason; Virginia: Amelia
    Bi-colored California: Pala
    Black tourmaline California: Pala; Georgia: LaGrange; Maine: Auburn, Bethel, Poland (GS), West Paris; New Hampshire: Grafton (I); North Carolina: Spruce Pine (FT)
    Gem tourmaline Maine: West Paris

Green tourmaline California: Pala; Maine: West Paris
Pink tourmaline California: Pala

Topaz (November Birthstone) Georgia: Cleveland (SA); Maine: Poland (GS); Montana: Helena; New Hampshire: Grafton (I); North Carolina (*): Almond, Boone, Cherokee, Franklin (2), Little Switzerland, Marion, Spruce Pine (3); Texas: Mason (2); Virginia: Amelia, McKenney
Pink topaz Washington: Ravensdale (GS)

Turquiose or Lapis Lazuli (December Birthstone)

Turquoise Nevada: Reno (GS)

Lapis Lazuli No listing

The preceding list of birthstones is taken from a list adopted in 1912 by the American National Association of Jewelers ("The Evolution of Birthstones" from *Jewelry & Gems—The Buying Guide* by Antoinette Matlins and A. C. Bonanno; GemStone Press, 2005).

Finding Your Anniversary Stone

The following is a listing of fee dig sites contained in this four-volume guide where you can find the stone that is associated with a particular anniversary.

First: Gold (Jewelry) Alabama: Cragford; Alaska: Anchorage, Chugach, Chicken, Copper Center, Fairbanks (3), Girdwood, Juneau, McGrath, Nome, Skagway (2), Talkeetna; Arizona: Apache Junction, Goldfield, Prescott, Wickenburg; California: Coloma, Columbia, Jackson, Jamestown, Mariposa, Nevada City, Pine Grove, Placerville; Colorado: Breckenridge, Granite, Idaho Springs (2), Ouray, Silverton; Georgia: Cleveland, Dahlonega (2), Gainesville; Indiana: Knightstown; Montana: Libby, Philipsburg; New Mexico: Gila; North Carolina: Cherokee, Marion (3), Midland, New London (2), Union Mills; Oregon: Baker City, Halfway, Jacksonville, Medford, Roseburg, Salem, Unity; South Dakota: Deadwood, Hill City, Keystone, Lead; Vermont: Plymouth; Virginia: Virginia City (SA)
Gold ore Colorado: Lakewood (M)

Second: Garnet Alaska: Juneau; Arizona: Tempe; California: Pala; Connecticut: Roxbury; Delaware: Wilmington; Georgia: Dahlonega (SA); Idaho: St. Maries; Maine: Auburn, Bethel, Poland (GS), West Paris; Montana: Alder, Helena (S); Nevada: Ely; New Hampshire: Grafton (I); New Mexico: Dixon; New York: North River; North Carolina (*): Almond, Boone, Canton, Cherokee, Chimney Rock, Franklin (4), Marshal, Hiddenite, Highlands, Little Switzerland (2), Marion, Spruce Pine (3) (FT); Tennessee: Ducktown; Texas: Mason; Virginia: McKenney, Virginia City (SA); Washington: Ravensdale (GS)
Almandine garnets Maine: Bethel, Poland (GS); Nevada: Ely
Pyrope garnets North Carolina: Franklin
Rhodolite garnets North Carolina: Franklin

Garnets, star Idaho: Moscow (GS), St. Maries

Third: Pearl No Listing

Fourth: Blue topaz No listing

Fifth: Sapphire Georgia: Cleveland (SA), Dahlonega (SA); Montana: Clinton (GS), Hamilton, Helena, Philipsburg (3); North Carolina (*): Almond, Cherokee, Franklin (8), Hiddenite, Highlands, Little Switzerland (2), Spruce Pine (2); Virginia: Virginia City (SA)
Sapphire, blue North Carolina: Canton
Sapphire, grey North Carolina: Canton
Sapphire, white North Carolina: Canton

Sapphire, bronze North Carolina: Canton
Sapphire, pink North Carolina: Canton
Star sapphire North Carolina: Boone (SA)

Sixth: Amethyst Arizona: Glendale; Arkansas: Mt. Ida (SA), Murfreesboro (S); Georgia: Cleveland; Maine: Bethel (R), West Paris; Montana: Dillon; Nevada: Reno (GS); New Hampshire: Grafton (I), Laconia; North Carolina (*): Almond, Boone, Cherokee, Chimney Rock, Franklin (3), Highlands, Little Switzerland, Spruce Pine (3); South Carolina: Antreville

Amethyst scepters Arizona: Tempe

Seventh: Onyx No listing

Eighth: Tourmaline Arizona: Tempe; California: Mesa Grande; Maine: Auburn (2), Poland (GS), West Paris; New Hampshire: Grafton (I); North Carolina (*): Boone, Franklin (2), Little Switzerland, Marion, Spruce Pine (3); Texas: Mason; Virginia: Amelia, McKenney
Bi-colored California: Pala
Black tourmaline California: Pala; Georgia: LaGrange; Maine: Auburn, Bethel, Poland (GS), West Paris; New Hampshire: Grafton (I); North Carolina: Spruce Pine (FT)
Gem tourmaline Maine: West Paris
Green tourmaline California: Pala; Maine: West Paris
Pink tourmaline California: Pala

Ninth: Lapis Lazuli No listing

Tenth: Diamond (Jewelry) Diamond Arkansas: Murfreesboro

Eleventh: Turquoise Nevada: Reno (GS)

Twelve: Jade No listing

Thirteenth: Citrine North Carolina (*): Almond, Boone, Cherokee, Franklin (3), Highlands, Little Switzerland, Spruce Pine (3)

Fourteenth: Opal
Black fire opal Nevada: Denio
Common opal New Mexico: Deming
Crystal opal Nevada: Denio
Fire opal Nevada: Denio (4), Reno (GS); Oregon: Klamath Falls
Hyalite opal Maine: Bethel
Precious opal Idaho: Spencer; Texas: Alpine
Virgin Valley opal Nevada: Reno (GS)
White opal Nevada: Denio
Wood opal Nevada: Denio

Fifteenth: Ruby Arkansas: Mt. Ida (SA); California: Pine Grove; Georgia: Cleveland, Dahlonega (SA); Montana: Helena; North Carolina (*): Almond, Boone, Cherokee, Chimney Rock, Franklin (8), Highlands, Little Switzerland (2), Spruce Pine (3); Virginia: Virginia City (SA)

Twentieth: Emerald Arkansas: Mt. Ida (SA); Georgia: Cleveland (SA), Dahlonega (SA); North Carolina (*): Almond, Boone, Cherokee, Chimney Rock, Franklin (2), Highlands, Little Switzerland (2), Marion, Micaville, Spruce Pine (2)
Crabtree emerald North Carolina: Spruce Pine

Twenty-fifth: Silver Michigan: Ontonagon

Thirtieth: Pearl No Listing

Thirty-fifth: Emerald Arkansas: Mt. Ida (SA); Georgia: Cleveland (SA), Dahlonega (SA); North Carolina (*): Almond, Boone, Cherokee, Chimney Rock, Franklin (2), Highlands, Little Switzerland (2), Marion, Micaville, Spruce Pine (2)
Crabtree emerald North Carolina: Spruce Pine

Fortieth: Ruby Arkansas: Mt. Ida (SA); California: Pine Grove; Georgia: Cleveland, Dahlonega (SA); Montana: Helena; North Carolina (*): Almond, Boone, Cherokee, Chimney Rock, Franklin (8), Highlands, Little Switzerland (2), Spruce Pine (3); Virginia: Virginia City (SA)

Forty-fifth: Sapphire Georgia: Cleveland (SA), Dahlonega (SA); Montana: Clinton (GS), Hamilton, Helena, Philipsburg (3); North Carolina (*): Almond, Cherokee, Franklin (8), Hiddenite, Highlands, Little Switzerland (2), Spruce Pine (2); Virginia: Virginia City (SA)
Sapphire, blue North Carolina: Canton
Sapphire, grey North Carolina: Canton
Sapphire, white North Carolina: Canton
Sapphire, bronze North Carolina: Canton
Sapphire, pink North Carolina: Canton
Star sapphire North Carolina: Boone (SA)

Fiftieth: Gold (*) Alabama: Cragford; Alaska: Anchorage, Chugach, Chicken, Copper Center, Fairbanks (3), Girdwood, Juneau, McGrath, Nome, Skagway (2), Talkeetna; Arizona: Apache Junction, Goldfield, Prescott, Wickenburg; California: Coloma, Columbia, Jackson, Jamestown, Mariposa, Nevada City, Pine Grove, Placerville; Colorado: Breckenridge, Granite, Idaho Springs (2), Ouray, Silverton; Georgia: Cleveland, Dahlonega (2), Gainesville; Indiana: Knightstown; Montana: Libby, Philipsburg; New Mexico: Gila; North Carolina: Cherokee, Marion (3), Midland, New London (2), Union Mills; Oregon: Baker City, Halfway, Jacksonville, Medford, Roseburg, Salem, Unity; South Dakota: Deadwood, Hill City, Keystone, Lead; Vermont: Plymouth; Virginia: Virginia City (SA)
Gold ore Colorado: Lakewood (M)

Fifty-fifth: Alexanderite No Listing

Sixtieth: Diamond Arkansas: Murfreesboro

Finding Your Zodiac Stone

The following is a listing of fee dig sites contained in this four-volume guide where you can find the stone that is associated with a particular zodiac sign. Refer to the individual mine listings for more information.

Aquarius (January 21–February 21) Garnet Alaska: Juneau; Arizona: Tempe; California: Pala; Connecticut: Roxbury; Delaware: Wilmington; Georgia: Dahlonega (SA); Idaho: St. Maries; Maine: Auburn, Bethel, Poland (GS), West Paris; Montana: Alder, Helena (S); Nevada: Ely; New Hampshire: Grafton (I); New Mexico: Dixon; New York: North River; North Carolina (*): Almond, Boone, Canton, Cherokee, Chimney Rock, Franklin (4), Marshal, Hiddenite, Highlands, Little Switzerland (2), Marion, Spruce Pine (3) (FT); Tennessee: Ducktown; Texas: Mason; Virginia: McKenney, Virginia City (SA); Washington: Ravensdale (GS)
  Almandine garnets Maine: Bethel, Poland (GS); Nevada: Ely
  Pyrope garnets North Carolina: Franklin
  Rhodolite garnets North Carolina: Franklin
  Garnets, star Idaho: Moscow (GS), St. Maries

Pisces (February 22–March 21) Amethyst Arizona: Glendale; Arkansas: Mt. Ida (SA), Murfreesboro (S); Georgia: Cleveland; Maine: Bethel (R), West Paris; Montana: Dillon; Nevada: Reno (GS); New Hampshire: Grafton (I), Laconia; North Carolina (*): Almond, Boone, Cherokee, Chimney Rock, Franklin (3), Highlands, Little Switzerland, Spruce Pine (3); South Carolina: Antreville
  Amethyst scepters Arizona: Tempe

Aries (March 22–April 20) Bloodstone (green chalcedony with red spots) No listing

Taurus (April 21–May 21) Sapphire Georgia: Cleveland (SA), Dahlonega (SA); Montana: Clinton (GS), Hamilton, Helena, Philipsburg (3); North Carolina (*): Almond, Cherokee, Franklin (8), Hiddenite, Highlands, Little Switzerland (2), Spruce Pine (2); Virginia: Virginia City (SA)
  Sapphire, blue North Carolina: Canton
  Sapphire, grey North Carolina: Canton
  Sapphire, white North Carolina: Canton
  Sapphire, bronze North Carolina: Canton
  Sapphire, pink North Carolina: Canton
  Star sapphire North Carolina: Boone (SA)

Gemini (May 22–June 21) Agate Arkansas: Murfreesboro (S); Michigan: Grand Marais; Montana: Helena (S); New Mexico: Deming; North Carolina: Chimney Rock; Oklahoma: Kenton (2); Oregon: Madras, Yachats; South Dakota: Wall; Texas: Three Rivers
Banded agate Texas: Alpine; New Mexico: Gila
Fire agate Arizona: Safford (2)
Iris agate Texas: Alpine
Ledge agate Oregon: Madras
Moss agate Oregon: Madras, Mitchell; Texas: Alpine (2); Wyoming: Shell
Polka-dot Jasp-agate Oregon: Madras
Plume agate Nevada: Reno (GS)
Pompom agate Texas: Alpine
Rainbow agate Oregon: Madras
Red plume agate Texas: Alpine

Cancer (June 22–July 22) Emerald Arkansas: Mt. Ida (SA); Georgia: Cleveland (SA), Dahlonega (SA); North Carolina (*): Almond, Boone, Cherokee, Chimney Rock, Franklin (2), Highlands, Little Switzerland (2), Marion, Micaville, Spruce Pine (2)
Crabtree emerald North Carolina: Spruce Pine

Leo (July 23–August 22) Onyx No listing

Virgo (August 23–September 22) Carnelian No Listing

Libra (September 23–October 23) Chrysolite or Peridot Chrysolite No listing
Peridot Arkansas: Murfreesboro (S); North Carolina (*): Boone, Chimney Rock, Franklin

Scorpio (October 24–November21) Beryl Delaware: Wilmington; Georgia: LaGrange; Maine: Auburn, Bethel, Poland (GS), West Paris; New Hampshire: Grafton (I); New Mexico: Dixon; North Carolina (*): Little Switzerland (2), Spruce Pine (2); Virginia: Amelia
Aqua beryl New Hampshire: Grafton (I)
Blue beryl (see also aquamarine) New Hampshire: Grafton (I)
Golden beryl North Carolina: Spruce Pine (FT); New Hampshire: Grafton (I)

Sagittarius (November 22–December 21) Topaz Georgia: Cleveland (SA); Maine: Poland (GS); Montana: Helena; New Hampshire: Grafton (I); North Carolina (*): Almond, Boone, Cherokee, Franklin (2), Little Switzerland, Marion, Spruce Pine (3); Texas: Mason (2); Virginia: Amelia
Pink topaz Washington: Ravensdale (GS)

Capricorn (December 22–January 21) Ruby Arkansas: Mt. Ida (SA); California: Pine Grove; Georgia: Cleveland, Dahlonega (SA); Montana: Helena; North Carolina (*): Almond, Boone, Cherokee, Chimney Rock, Franklin (8), Highlands, Little Switzerland (2), Spruce Pine (3); Virginia: Virginia City (SA)

The preceding list of zodiacal stones has been passed on from an early Hindu legend (taken from *Jewelry & Gems—The Buying Guide* by Antoinette Matlins and A. C. Bonanno; GemStone Press, 2005).

The following is an old Spanish list, probably representing Arab traditions, which ascribes the following stones to various signs of the zodiac (taken from *Jewelry & Gems— The Buying Guide* by Antoinette Matlins and A. C. Bonanno; GemStone Press, 2005).

Aquarius (January 21–February 21) Amethyst Arizona: Glendale; Arkansas: Mt. Ida (SA), Murfreesboro (S); Georgia: Cleveland; Maine: Bethel (R), West Paris; Montana: Dillon; Nevada: Reno (GS); New Hampshire: Grafton (I), Laconia; North Carolina (*): Almond, Boone, Cherokee, Chimney Rock, Franklin (3), Highlands, Little Switzerland, Spruce Pine (3); South Carolina: Antreville
Amethyst scepters Arizona: Tempe

Pisces (February 22–March 21) Undistinguishable

Aries (March 22–April 20) Quartz Arizona: Glendale (GS), Tempe; Arkansas: Jessieville (3), Mt. Ida (6) (Y), Murfreesboro (S), Pencil Bluff, Story (2); California: Pine Grove; Delaware: Wilmington; Georgia: Lincolnton; Illinois: Hamilton; Maine: Auburn, Poland (GS), West Paris; Michigan: Ontonagon; Montana: Dillon, Helena (S); New Hampshire: Laconia; New Mexico: Bingham, Deming, Dixon; North Carolina: Franklin; Texas: Alpine, Mason; Virginia: Amelia, Virginia City (SA); Washington: Ravensdale (GS)
Blue Georgia: Lincolnton; North Carolina: Marion
Clear Georgia: LaGrange; North Carolina (*): Hiddenite, Little Switzerland, Marion, Spruce Pine
Milky Maine: Bethel
Parallel growth Maine: West Paris
Pseudocubic crystals Maine: West Paris
Rose Maine: Bethel; New Hampshire: Grafton (I); North Carolina (*): Franklin
Rutilated North Carolina (*): Little Switzerland, Spruce Pine
Skeletal quartz South Carolina: Antreville
Smoky Maine: Bethel; Nevada: Reno (GS); New Hampshire: Grafton, Laconia; North Carolina (*): Almond, Boone, Cherokee, Chimney Rock, Franklin (4), Hiddenite, Highlands, Little Switzerland (2), Marion, Spruce Pine (2); Virginia: McKenney
Smoky (gem quality) New Hampshire: Grafton (I); South Carolina: Antreville
Quartz "diamonds"
Lake Co. "diamonds" (moon tears) California; Lake County
Cape May "diamonds" New Jersey: Cape May
Herkimer "diamonds" New York: Herkimer, Middleville, St. Johnsville
Taurus (April 21–May 21) Rubies, Diamonds

Rubies Arkansas: Mt. Ida (SA); California: Pine Grove; Georgia: Cleveland, Dahlonega (SA); Montana: Helena; North Carolina (*): Almond, Boone, Cherokee, Chimney Rock, Franklin (8), Highlands, Little Switzerland (2), Spruce Pine (3);Virginia: Virginia City (SA)

Diamond Arkansas: Murfreesboro;

Gemini (May 22–June 21) Sapphire
Georgia: Cleveland (SA), Dahlonega (SA); Montana: Clinton (GS), Hamilton, Helena, Philipsburg (3); North Carolina (*): Almond, Cherokee, Franklin (8), Hiddenite, Highlands, Little Switzerland (2), Spruce Pine (2); Virginia: Virginia City (SA)

Sapphire, blue North Carolina: Canton
Sapphire, grey North Carolina: Canton
Sapphire, white North Carolina: Canton
Sapphire, bronze North Carolina: Canton
Sapphire, pink North Carolina: Canton
Star sapphire North Carolina: Boone (SA)

Cancer (June 22–July 22) Agate and Beryl
Agate Arkansas: Murfreesboro (S); Michigan: Grand Marais; Montana: Helena (S); New Mexico: Deming; North Carolina: Chimney Rock; Oklahoma: Kenton (2); Oregon: Madras, Yachats; South Dakota: Wall; Texas: Three Rivers

Banded agate Texas: Alpine; New Mexico: Gila
Fire agate Arizona: Safford (2)
Iris agate Texas: Alpine
Ledge agate Oregon: Madras
Moss agate Oregon: Madras, Mitchell; Texas: Alpine (2); Wyoming: Shell
Polka-dot Jasp-agate Oregon: Madras
Plume agate Nevada: Reno (GS)
Pompom agate Texas: Alpine
Rainbow agate Oregon: Madras
Red plume agate Texas: Alpine
Beryl Delaware: Wilmington; Georgia: LaGrange; Maine: Auburn, Bethel, Poland (GS), West Paris; New Hampshire: Grafton (I); New Mexico: Dixon; North Carolina (*): Little Switzerland (2), Spruce Pine (2); Virginia: Amelia

Aqua beryl New Hampshire: Grafton (I)
Blue beryl (see also aquamarine) New Hampshire: Grafton (I)
Golden beryl North Carolina: Spruce Pine (FT); New Hampshire: Grafton (I)

Leo (July 23–August 22) Topaz
Georgia: Cleveland (SA); Maine: Poland (GS); Montana: Helena; New Hampshire: Grafton (I); North Carolina (*): Almond, Boone, Cherokee, Franklin (2), Little Switzerland, Marion, Spruce Pine (3); Texas: Mason (2); Virginia: Amelia

Pink topaz Washington: Ravensdale (GS)

Virgo (August 23–September 22) Bloodstone (green chalcedony with red spots)
No listing

Libra (September 23–October 23) Jasper Arkansas: Murfreesboro (S); California: Pine Grove; Montana: Helena (S); Oklahoma: Kenton; Oregon: Madras, Yachats; Texas: Alpine

Jasper braccia New Mexico: Gila
Brown Jasper New Mexico: Deming
Chocolate jasper New Mexico: Deming
Orange jasper New Mexico: Deming
Picture jasper New Mexico: Gila; Oregon: Mitchell
Pink jasper New Mexico: Deming
Variegated jasper New Mexico: Deming
Yellow jasper New Mexico: Deming, Gila

Scorpio (October 24–November 21) Garnet Alaska: Juneau; Arizona: Tempe; California: Pala; Connecticut: Roxbury; Deleware: Wilmington; Georgia: Dahlonega (SA); Idaho: St. Maries; Maine: Auburn, Bethel, Poland (GS), West Paris; Montana: Alder, Helena (S); Nevada: Ely; New Hampshire: Grafton (I); New Mexico: Dixon; New York: North River; North Carolina (*): Almond, Boone, Canton, Cherokee, Chimney Rock, Franklin (4), Marshal, Hiddenite, Highlands, Little Switzerland (2), Marion, Spruce Pine (3) (FT); Tennessee: Ducktown; Texas: Mason; Virginia: McKenney, Virginia City (SA); Washington: Ravensdale (GS)

Almandine garnets Maine: Bethel, Poland (GS); Nevada: Ely
Pyrope garnets North Carolina: Franklin
Rhodolite garnets North Carolina: Franklin

Sagittarius (November 22–December 21) Emerald Arkansas: Mt. Ida (SA); Georgia: Cleveland (SA), Dahlonega (SA); North Carolina (*): Almond, Boone, Cherokee, Chimney Rock, Franklin (2), Highlands, Little Switzerland (2), Marion, Micaville, Spruce Pine (2)

Crabtree emerald North Carolina: Spruce Pine

Capricorn (December 22–January 21) Chalcedony Arizona: Safford; Nevada: Reno (GS); New Mexico: Demin

Some Publications on Gems and Minerals

Jewelry Artist
(Lapidary Journal)
300 Chesterfield Parkway, Suite 100
Malvern, PA 19355
Phone: (610) 232-5700
Subscriptions: (800) 676-4336
www.lapidaryjournal.com

Rocks & Minerals
c/o Heldref Publications
1319 18th Street, NW
Washington, DC 20036-1802
Subscriptions: (866) 802-7059

Rock & Gem
c/o Miller Magazines, Inc.
Maple Court, Suite 232
Ventura, CA 93003-3517
www.rockngem.com

Gold Prospector
Gold Prospectors Association of
America, Inc.
43445 Business Park Drive
Temecula, CA 92590
Phone: (800) 551-9707
www.goldprospectors.org

Colored Stone
300 Chesterfield Parkway, Suite 100
Malvern, PA 19355
Phone: (610) 232-5700
www.colored-stone.com

The Mineralogical Record
P.O. Box 35565
Tucson, AZ 85740
Phone: (520) 297-6709
Fax: (520) 544-0815
www.mineralogicalrecord.com

Other sources of information are local and regional rock, gem, and mineral clubs and federations, and rock, gem, and mineral shows. Many times clubs offer field trips and some shows have collecting trips associated with their annual event. Among these are The American Federation of Mineralogical Societies (www.amfed.org), which lists member clubs, and Bob's Rock Shop (www.rockhounds.com), which has a U.S. club directory (supplied information).

Send Us Your Feedback

Disclaimer

The authors have made every reasonable effort to obtain accurate information for this guide. However, much of the information in the book is based on material provided by the sites and has not been verified independently. The information given here does not represent recommendations, but merely a listing of information. The authors and publisher accept no liability for any accident or loss incurred when readers are patronizing the establishments listed herein. The authors and publisher accept no liability for errors or omissions. Since sites may shut down or change their hours of operations or fees without advance notice, please call the site before your visit for confirmation before planning your trip.

The authors would appreciate being informed of changes, additions, or deletions that should be made to this guide. To that end, a form is attached, which can be filled out and mailed to the authors for use in future editions of the guide.

Have We Missed Your Mine or Museum?

This is a project with a national scope, based on extensive literature search, phone and mail inquiry, and personal investigation. However, we are dealing with a business in which many owners are retiring or closing and selling their sites. In addition, many of the mines, guide services, and smaller museums have limited publicity, known more by word of mouth than by publication. Thus, it is possible that your operation or one you have visited was not included in this guide. Please let us know if you own or operate a mine, guide service, or museum, or have visited a mine, guide service, or museum that is not in the guide. It will be considered for inclusion in the next edition of the guide. Send updates to:

Treasure Hunter's Guides
GemStone Press
Route 4, Sunset Farm Offices
P.O. Box 237
Woodstock, VT 05091

Do You Have a Rockhounding Story to Share?

If you have a special story about a favorite dig site, send it in for consideration for use in the next edition of the guide.

A Request to Mines and Museums:

For sites already included in this guide, we request that you put us on your annual mailing list so that we may have an updated copy of your information.

Notes on Museums

In this guide we have included listings of museums with noteworthy gem, mineral, or rock collections. We particularly tried to find local museums displaying gems or minerals native to the area where they are located. This list is by no means complete, and if you feel we missed an important listing, let us know by completing the following form. Since these guides focus specifically on gems and minerals, only those exhibits have been recognized in the museum listings, and we do not mention any collection or exhibits of fossils. See our sequel on fossils for information on fossil collections.

READER'S CONTRIBUTION

I would like to supply the following information for possible inclusion in the next edition of *The Treasure Hunter's Guide*:

Type of entry: ☐ fee dig ☐ guide service ☐ museum ☐ mine tour ☐ annual event

This is a: ☐ new entry ☐ entry currently in the guide

Nature of info: ☐ addition ☐ change ☐ deletion

Please describe (brochure and additional info may be attached):

_____

_____

_____

_____

Please supply the following in case we need to contact you regarding your information:

Name: _____

Address: _____

_____

_____

Phone: (____) _____

E-mail: _____

Date: _____

FIELD NOTES

FIELD NOTES

FIELD NOTES

FIELD NOTES

FIELD NOTES

FIELD NOTES

FIELD NOTES

FIELD NOTES

FIELD NOTES

FIELD NOTES

FIELD NOTES

FIELD NOTES

FIELD NOTES